No mistakes Only Lessons

How to enjoy the journey in such a messy world

Pendragon Tim Chng

This publication is designed to provide competent information regarding the subject matter covered. It is sold with the understanding that the author and publisher are not engaged in rendering legal, financial, medical, or any other professional advice.

Laws and practices often vary from state to state, and from country to country. They are also subject to change. If any expert advice is required, then the services of a professional should be sought.

The author and publisher specifically disclaim any liability that may incurred from the use or application of the contents of this publication.

You may like to visit Quora where the author is actively engaged.

To

Mui Ann

my beloved wife and best friend

who stood by me through thick and thin

and to my wonderfully supportive children

Christopher, Jonathan, Veronica & Yvonne

who cheered me on.

Also by Pendragon Tim Chng

The Way of the Tortoise

The 7 Mistakes Winners Don't Make

Financial Bootcamp

Cheerful at Age 100

The 7 Roads Less Traveled

Parents Alert

Happiness Shortcuts

Sun Tzu's Art of War

CONTENTS

Chapter Ten
Cyber insecurity

INTRODUCTION

HELPLESSNESS is the worst emotion you can feel right now. You know you are in danger but you can't do much about it. Bad news keep attacking all of us - a novel coronavirus, memories about the Spanish flu pandemic (1918 - 1920) that wiped out 50 million people, US-China 21st century war, US-Iran war, a highly probable coming market crash worst then the 1929 market crash, assassinations, violent protests, fraud is everywhere - in religion, finance, government, the medical sector, and ***a pressure-cooker life that leads to the breakdown of the family***...bad news keep coming.

What shall we do?

Now is the time for family and friends to come together as one. Unity is strength. But it is not possible to walk together unless you share the same vision, care about the same things, and have the same answers to these most important questions:

- How can I enjoy the journey in such a messy world?
- How would the US-China 21st century war impact my life?
- How can I take my life back from corporate dominance?
- How do good people make tough decisions?
- What is a wise definition of success?

You don't have to reinvent the wheel. I've already done that for YOU! If you want to ENJOY THE JOURNEY, you need this HANDBOOK. It will provide all the answers to these urgent questions. To love each other more, stop quarreling. Embrace this beautiful concept - in life, there are NO MISTAKES, ONLY LESSONS!

Complexity simplified

Oliver Wendell Holmes, Supreme Court Judge, appointed by former US President Theodore Roosevelt said:

I would not give a fig for the simplicity this side of complexity, but I would give my life for the simplicity on the other side of complexity.

Our world may be described as volatile, uncertain, complex, ambiguous, dangerous and highly competitive. It follows therefore that parochial, sectarian and simplistic strategies cannot help us solve personal or global problems.

MAKING WISE DECISIONS is the most powerful tool for you to control your destiny. To simplify complexity in life, you begin by wisely thinking about how you make decisions.

HOW IMPORTANT ARE THE DECISIONS YOU MAKE?

Decisions have the power to steer and change your life forever. Therefore, nothing affects the quality of your life more than your ability to make the right decisions. All that you have achieved or failed to achieved can be traced back to the decisions you've made - on issues concerning your vote, health, wealth, relationships, and life purpose.

In his book, ***BLINK, the power of thinking without thinking***, Malcolm Gladwell proves that great decision-makers aren't those who process the most information or spend the most time deliberating, but those who have perfected the art of "thin-sli-

cing" - knowing the very few things that matter.
Therefore if you want to enjoy the journey, you must make a firm DECISION to turn your mistakes into valuable lessons. So your focus should be to look for opportunities to grow in any crisis instead of getting depressed. Growing from your mistakes is what matters most.

This is the awesome attitude that will make your nation and family great again. As Goethe commented wisely - that which matter most must never be at the mercy of things that matter least.

To learn lessons from your mistakes and also to make your nation and family great, you must gather the best practices of great nations and great civilizations in their prime, from anywhere in the world.

In such a quest, you will cross man-made borders to seek truth from facts. You need to practice creative destruction, dumping ideas that are parochial, sectarian, obsolete, and inefficient and embracing new creative ideas regardless of race, language or religion.

You have unconsciously stumbled on the natural process of hybridization - the proactive evolution of remarkable solutions to man's challenges, making full use of the latest breakthroughs in technology, science, the humanities, and the art of governance.

In any mission to be undertaken, whether it is military or any other endeavor, you must be clear what your objective is. You must focus on how to make your nation and family great again by turning your mistakes into lessons. In this way, you're evolving into a higher human being.

This is what matter most. It would be foolish to focus on ideology. As a wise person once said; Every success has a seed of failure. What works today may not work tomorrow. People, circumstances and many other factors are constantly evolving.

But it would be wise to focus on RESULTS that people want. We seek out the principles that will bring peace and prosperity to the people.

That which matter most must never be at the mercy of things that matter least. We must put first things first and last things last.

Our main objective is to bring POSITIVE RESULTS to the people. If we stray from this, then we have failed the people.

When we fail to produce positive results for our nation and family, the right decision to make is to change our ideology and methodology rather than becoming more stubborn and more hard line, kowtowing to our dogma.

Why is this so?

This is because wisdom always take the longer term view of spiritual growth. Wisdom avoids knee-jerk reactions to situations you're in right now.

Wisdom is usually counter-intuitive and less self-centered. Wisdom is focusing on others in the community as well.

Wisdom switches from dogma to principles, seeing the big picture.

Community over self is wiser than individualism. Achieving RESULTS is wiser than protecting your dogma. Community action is far more effective then individual actions because unity is strength. A lone ranger is weak. Win-win solutions are easier to achieve than win-lose solutions.
For example, the progress of Modern China as a super power was not achieved by Sun Yat-sen or Mao Zidong but by Deng Xiaoping who provided two great gems of wisdom to prosper China:

- Whether the cat is black or white makes no difference. A cat that catches mice is a good cat. (Whether it is communism or not makes no difference. A government that bring prosperity to the people is a good government).

- To be rich is glorious for it is proper that man should find ways to improve his quality of life. (democratic capitalism that is not predatory)

Sun Yat-sen was ineffective because he used western ideas for an Asian country. Mao Zidong was ineffective because he took a hard line on dogma just like the Americans and not on producing results for the people.

So the most important takeaway from this discussion is that there is a spiritual war between RESULTS versus dogma.

So if you have to argue, win the argument by talking about RESULTS when people talk about dogma.

So when people try to differentiate the Americans from the Chinese, talking about democracy and communism is unproductive and down right foolish. It is a big waste of precious time because it is putting the cart before the horse. The horse represents Results. The type of carriage is less important.

A system that brings tangible RESULTS to the people is a good system.

Humility the key to lifelong learning

We can all relate to the fact that there will be no gain when there is no pain. There will be no skill when there is no drill. This is how the hardware and the software of human beings operate.

It is through pain and drill that man evolves upwards.

So here are a few examples of why we must seek wisdom. The master virtue that make us wise is humility. Humility is the willingness to accept constructive criticism without anger and learn the lessons of life. Arrogance is refusing to self-examine for possible errors in our attitude, habits, and paradigm.

We will continue to suffer pain until we are humble enough to acknowledge we'd made a mistake and we are willing to learn our lesson. It is wise to embrace the notion that in life there are no mistakes, only lessons.

Albert Einstein says that insanity is doing the same thing over and over again and expecting different results. No problem can be solved at the same level of consciousness that produces that mistake.

Let's take this example. John Sununu had a high IQ but was not humble. He believed, wrongly, that IQ was what mattered and he did not keep his high IQ a secret. As White House chief of staff under former President George Bush, he made many enemies in Congress with his arrogant behavior. For example, he publicly belittled Senator Trent Lott, calling him "insignificant." Later, Lott became a member of the Senate Republican leadership. Sununu had great difficulty in getting cooperation from Lott.

Despite his genius-level IQ, Sununu made a mistake so foolish, it led to his professional suicide. He used military planes to go around the country on personal and political errands, neglecting the fact that his actions and wasting taxpayers hundreds of thousands of dollars was not lawful.

Calls for his resignation arose in Congress and he needed defenders fast. No one came forth to help him because of his arrogance. In fact, legions of Congress insiders took this opportunity to stick knives into him.

Harvard and Stanford are fertile breeding grounds for superbrain arrogance. They pontificate in the ivory towers of academia without real experience in the battlefields.They were also billing the US government for items that had nothing to do with government projects. Stanford President Donald Kennedy bought a 72-foot yacht, spent on a reception for his new wife and put them on the US government account. He was forced to resign.

Smart people do dumb things because of arrogance and its related tendencies of isolation, recklessness, and overreaching. Smart people fail because they boast about their IQ but neglect the development oftheir social skills, civility, simple common sense, self-knowledge, and character.

The mindset (internal pictures, beliefs, attitudes, mental state, mental models, vision and so forth) and the opening statements of a humble person and that of an arrogant person are as different as night and day.

A humble person may begin his conversation in this friendly win-win way, treating others as equals: “I would like to know what is your reasoning behind your decision...I just like to understand you better.”

An arrogant person may begin his conversation with assumptions and accusation: “Why did you make such a stupid mistake...don’t make excuses...”

Learning something new and useful may require you to take the risk of moving out of your comfort zone, away from your old habits, race, language, religion, country, and professional expertise.

It is so tempting to follow the example of the drunkard who had lost his keys at night somewhere but insisted on looking for them under the lamp post because the light is better here.

This story may be a joke but we find it funny because it is all too true. Biases such as sectarianism and our dogma lead us to looking for information that is most readily available, easiest to process, the most understandable, and within our discipline.

Don’t make the mistake of failing to embrace the whole truth and the longer term view. Don't foolishly cherry-pick information to suit your unsubstantiated claims. That is why argument is not meant to be constructive. Argument is usually obstructive to making good decisions.

How can we learn anything new when we are so arrogant as to believe we already know everything.

Once upon a time, a young man wanted to be a Samurai swordsman. He trained hard and indeed became a Samurai swordsman. But he wanted to be the top Samurai swordsman, a gold medalist.

The young Samurai swordsman entered the house of a famous Zen master. He bowed respectfully and said, "Master! I have mastered the highest level of Zen, both in theory and in practice. I have been training for many years. I heard that you are great. Therefore I come here to bow to you and hope you can teach me something."

The Zen master looked at this proud young Samurai swordsman. Without a word, he went to the back room and brought out a tray, a teapot filled with hot tea and a teacup and placed them on a table. He invited him to sit with him at the table. He placed the teacup in front of the proud young man and started pouring tea into the teacup.

Soon the teacup was full and started to overflow. But the Zen master did not stop pouring. The young man looked at the Zen master with a confused expression. The proud young swordsman said, "Stop, master!"

The Zen master said, "This is you. You are too full already. I cannot teach you. If you want to learn, you must first empty your cup."

Can you be humble?

Who knows what's good what's bad

Ancient Chinese wisdom is encrypted in the Chinese language. The two Chinese characters for the word CRISIS are DANGER and OPPORTUNITY. It is part of the philosophy behind Sun Tzu's ***The Art of War***.

Crisis, danger, and opportunity coexist together, always.

Wisdom means seeking opportunities every time there is a problem. Entrepreneurs know this wisdom best. When there is a big problem and you can solve it quickly for people, you will have a big opportunity to make big profits.

It follows therefore that whenever there is a problem, approach this problem with a POSITIVE MENTAL ATTITUDE. Treat every crisis, problem or mistake as an OPPORTUNITY to do something proactive and positive. Say something like this whenever a crisis or problem crops up;

"Now, we've got a chance to do something..."

This is parallel to the great concept taught by Cherie Carter-Scott;

In life, there are no mistakes, only lessons.

Arrogance interferes with our attempt to seek wisdom. Putting our ego on our throne makes us do dumb things.

Therefore any method or technology that can design away the stupid ego is worth mastering - such as ***Six Thinking Hats*** by Edward de Bono, the Harvard professor that save mankind from the stupid habit of argument.

Arrogance blinds us to the fact that the future is not as predictable as smart people would have you believe. In other words, you will be smarter than smart people when you can sincerely utter "Who knows what's good and what's bad."

Many a times, bad things happen which can turn out to be blessings in disguise. We have to see the big picture, seeing the trees and the forest. Bad things that happened to us can be viewed wisely as opportunities to learn something useful to be applied in the future.

You may hope for the best but you must always be prepared for the worst.

The expression "You can't see the forest for the trees" means that we cannot see the situations as they really are while we are in the midst of them.

This expression is similar to what Albert Einstein - You can't solve a problem at the same level of consciousness that created this problem.

Maybe you have to get away to gain a better perspective. Like a sniper, you want to position yourself at a better vantage point to view your target.

Maybe you have to get at least one other thinking person to bounce ideas around to arrive at the best decisions.

Once upon a time in ancient China there lived an old Chinese farmer. Unlike other farmers in this small village, he had a horse.

One day, the old farmer's horse ran away. His neighbor came running to him and said, "I'm so sorry about your horse."

The old farmer said, "Who knows what's good and what's bad."

His neighbor was confused because a horse was a valuable asset, and losing it was a terrible loss.

But one day, his horse returned with another horse.

His neighbor came running to him and said, "Congratulations

on your great fortune."

The old farmer said, "Who knows what's good and what's bad."

Again his neighbor was confused, because having an additional horse was good fortune.

The next day, the old farmer's son rode the new horse to tame it. He was thrown down and he broke his leg.

His neighbor came running to him and said, "I'm so sorry about your son."

The old farmer said, "Who knows what's good and what's bad."

Again his neighbor was rather confused. Surely having a son with a broken leg isn't a happy occasion.

The next day, the army came to the small village to conscript able-bodied young men to go and fight a war. But the old farmer's son was exempted - because he had a broken leg.

Six blind men and an elephant

To be wiser, you should use a big globe rather than the world map printed on an A1 paper. The world is round not flat. China is both east and west of the United States.

To be wiser, we need to move out of our comfort zone to probe more deeply elsewhere, maybe in other countries, discipline, race, language, religion and civilization. That is why traveling to unfamiliar places can be very illuminating. Working in a foreign land is even more educational and enlightening.

There is an ancient story from India that has many versions. One of these versions goes like this.

Six blind men wanted to conceptualize the elephant. So they were brought to touch and feel an elephant. The first blind man touched the side of the elephant and exclaimed, "The elephant is like a wall."

The second blind man touched the leg of the elephant and exclaimed, "No, no, no. The elephant is like a tree trunk."

The third blind man touched the ear of the elephant, and exclaimed, "Both of you are wrong. The elephant is like a big fan."

The fourth blind men touched the tusk of the elephant, and exclaimed, "All three of you are wrong. The elephant is like a spear."

The fifth blind men touched the trunk of the elephant and exclaimed, "No, no, no. The elephant is like a python."

The sixth blind man touched the tail of the elephant., and exclaimed, "All of you are wrong. The elephant is like a rope."

In actual truth, the elephant is all of the above and much much more.

If you believe in the validity of the foregoing, then you will assess the statements made by US Vice President Mike Pence as rather parochial. When one NBA staff tweeted support for the Hong Kong violent protesters, China took issue. Mike Pence commented that we should not kowtow to China.

What?

Support for the freedom of speech without the mention of personal responsibility, the rule of law (lawfulness), and due process?

So it's ok to say out loud that a lady is fat because she is fat?

What about good manners and civility?

In this case, if we have nothing constructive or kind to say, we should keep our big mouth shut.

Yes, we should not kowtow to China. I totally agree. We should at the same time not kowtow to the United States as well. We should all kowtow to PRINCIPLES, VALUES & VIRTUES. Principles, values, and virtues in turn will determine where the red lines are and what behavior is not acceptable anywhere, neither in China, the United States nor any other nation.

Behavior that most countries will find unacceptable are:

- Corruption
- Incompetence
- Ingratitude
- Cruelty
- Rudeness
- Kicking a puppy
- Abusing the homeless
- Becoming a lawless vigilante.
- Making racist remarks
- Interfering in the internal affairs of other countries

Our behavior emanates from our beliefs

Psychology 101 provides the big picture of human nature. Basic psychology teaches us that how we behave is dependent on what we believe.

It is our set of beliefs that produces our values. These values will galvanize our attitudes, which in turn result in the way we think, behave, speak, react, plan and live. Each of these verbs generate the many decisions we make everyday.

What does this means?

It means - change your belief and you change your life.

Why?

Because your beliefs are the building blocks of your reality, your life.

So if you want to make the right decisions, you have to list down all your beliefs and do some creative destruction - rejecting all beliefs that are working against you and accentuating beliefs or cultivating new beliefs that will ***make you, your family, and your nation great again.***

In his book, ***BLINK - the power of thinking without thinking***, Malcolm Gladwell reveals that great decision-makers aren't those who process the most information or spend the most time deliberating, but those who have perfected the art of "thin slicing" - knowing the very few things that matter.

Change your beliefs, and you will change your principles, values, virtues, habits, attitudes, social skills, ethics, behavior and so forth.

In life there are no mistakes, only lessons. The secret to resilience, happiness and a less stressful success is to avoid focusing on stagnant traits. Instead, focus on adopting an active, growth-oriented and problem-solving approach to life, and enjoying the journey together with your loved ones.

Here are the beliefs of greatness that will empower you to enjoy the journey with your loved ones:

- That which is hateful to you, do not do to your fellow

human beings. Any interpretation of scriptures that bred hatred or disdain for others - whatever their beliefs - is illegitimate. (Hillel)

- True religion is protecting the powerless - orphans, widows, homeless, migrant workers, disabled, and injured soldiers returning from an unnecessary war. (Scriptures)

- Power without love is reckless and abusive. Love without power is sentimental and anemic. Power at its best is love implementing the demands of justice. Justice at its best is power correcting everything that stands against love. (Martin Luther King)

- That which matter most must never be at the mercy of things that matter least. (Goethe)

- Courage is not the absence of fear but rather the judgment that something is more important than fear. The brave may not live forever. But the cautious do not live at all. (Meg Cabot)

- So long as you open your heart to beauty, hope, cheer, courage and power, so long are you young. (Samuel Ulman). I know of no more encouraging fact than the unquestionable ability of man to elevate his life by conscious endeavor (Henry David Thoreau).

- We should encourage each other to follow the rules of considerate conduct such as think before we act, listen more, argue less, seek first to understand, think twice before asking favors, avoid shifting responsibility and blame, avoid jumping to conclusions, respect other's opinion, and enjoying the journey with your loved ones.

- If you want to achieve what you've never achieved before, you have to grow to become what you've never become before. (Brian Tracy). Insanity is doing the same over and over again and expecting different results. No problem can be solved at the same level of consciousness that created it. (Albert Einstein)

- Success and cheerfulness in life are not the result of what we have but rather how we live. What we do with the things we already have now makes the biggest difference in the quality of our life. (Tony Robbins)
- Studies have shown that companies hire for attitude and train for skills. (Singapore Airlines).
- Humility is the beginning of wisdom. (Zen habits)
- A foolish definition of success is the attainment of a certain amount of money, power, and privilege. A wise definition of success is enjoying the journey of lifelong learning with your loved ones.
- All men are created equal, endowed with the unalienable rights to life, liberty and the pursuit of happiness. (US Declaration of Independence)
- The world will be safer and prosperous when all nations adhere to the principles of peaceful coexistence where there is mutual respect for each other's territorial sovereignty and the right to self-determination and non-interference. (China-India)
- Whether a cat is black or white makes no difference. A cat that catches mice is a good cat. Whether we label an ideology socialism, capitalism, communism, or authoritarianism makes no difference. A government that can provide affordable subsidized public housing, meaningful jobs, efficient transport system, clean environment, fantastic schools, universal health care, recreation centers, and national security is a good government and should be given a strong mandate to govern. (Deng Xiaoping)
- Every nation must strive to avoid contracting the na-

tional disease of schizophrenia. A nation suffers schizophrenia when there are two equally dominant sectarian political parties, bickering with each other like two juveniles. It is best if there is a political party that promote universal values that protect the rights of minorities so as to gain at least 70% of popular vote thus attaining a strong mandate to govern.

- Workers must enjoy democracy at the workplace where they have a say in the management of the company and reserve the right to buy the company if the owners decide to sell.
- All citizens must have a fair share in the prosperity of the nation. This can be achieved by practicing universal basic income (UBI) calculated as a small percentage of the living wage. UBI is able to soften the ills of neoliberalism by reducing the pain and frustration of the underprivileged who are the victims of the wealth gap between the rich and the poor. UBI is able to reduce the risk of violent civil unrest.
- Every citizen must be given universal healthcare.
- Every person has the right to demand privacy, especially when he or she has not committed any crime. (Edward Snowden)
- Every person has the right to choose his own way of life without being judged or criticized so long as he or she respects the rule of law. He can choose voluntary simplicity, country living, living off the grid, any profession, urban competition, climbing the corporate ladder, activism, the military, or politics.
- Whistleblowers should be protected by law when they expose the wrongdoings within the company or government.

Repetition boosts learning

One of the aims of the foregoing discussion is to set the tone for this handbook. To enjoy the journey with your loved ones, you have to live by your values, virtues, principles, and beliefs of greatness.

Practice makes perfect. The reason why we need to practice is that repetition makes us learn. Whether it is shooting the basket in basketball, playing the piano, parallel park your car, or memorizing a maxim, you need to repeat and repeat until it becomes a habit.

The average human brain is made up of 86 billion neurons (nerve cells or brain cells). These are specialized cells with dendrites and long axons. Neurons talk with each other using electrochemical signals called action potentials. Signals will travel from one neuron to the next neuron crossing a microscopic gap called a synapse. Each neuron can connect with up to 10,000 other neurons by that number of dendritic endings.

So a synapse is a special junction between two dendrites of two neuron. At this location, ions with a positive or negative charge will be interacting with excitatory neurotransmitters (e.g. acetylcholine, glutamate, aspartate, noradrenaline, histamine) and inhibitory neurotransmitters (e.g. GABA, glycine, serotonin). These interactions will result in the actions required such as encoding, consolidation, storage and retrieval of memories.

When you perform an action, such as ***memorizing a belief of greatness,*** it fires off many electrochemical signals which form a network. Old synapses are cleared away to highlight the new connections. After much repetition, it becomes internalized as an unique pattern in your brain in the form of a unit of memory, which you can retrieve anytime.

To improve your memorization, spaced out your practice, preferably daily. But be careful. If you practice the wrong pattern, that will be memorized wrongly. So it is perfect practice that makes perfect.

Learning is also boosted by viewing a maxim from another angle. It sharpens our understanding of truth and reality.

Aristotle said:

We are what we repeatedly do. Excellence, then, is not an act, but a habit.

When you internalize a belief of greatness (e.g. what is true religion), by repetition, it becomes a part of you. It becomes a habit of thought:

Little drops of water
Tiny grains of sand
Make a mighty ocean
And a pleasant land.

Your character is a composite of your habits. Your habits comes from embracing a set of beliefs of greatness, repeated so many times that it becomes part of your subconscious. The subconscious then directs your tendencies to make decisions based on such beliefs which collectively is called wisdom.

This is how wise people make decisions.

As we focus on making every mistake into a valuable lesson, we become older and wiser. This is how you achieve greatness - in yourself, in your family, and in your nation.

Enjoying the journey

Even though we are enjoying the journey, in an odyssey of lifelong learning from our mistakes, be prepared for ***a long and bumpy ride.*** Therefore, be prepared to tough it out to the very end.

Never ever give up part way. If you are already halfway there, don't ever turn around and go back. Don't rely on your talents, genius, education, or money. Let your spirit lead you.

PRESS ON with hope in your heart and you'll never walk alone, for we are with you all the way:

Former president Calvin Coolidge says it best:

Nothing can take the place of ***PERSISTENCE.***
Talent will not.
Nothing is as common as unsuccessful people with talent.
Genius will not.
Unrewarded genius is almost a proverb.
Education will not.
The world is full of educated derelicts.
*The slogan "**PRESS ON!**" has solved and always will solve*
The problems of the human race.

To help you keep going when the going gets tough, always remember that ***you'll never walk alone.*** Hum this song, and soon others who are sharing the same pain and struggles of life as you, will join you in spirit, in song, and in taking action to pursue the same vision of a better world.

You'll Never Walk Alone is a show tune from the 1945 Rodgers & Hammerstein musical ***Carousel***. In the second act of the musical, Nettie Fowler, the cousin of the protagonist Julie Jordan, sings ***"You'll Never Walk alone"*** to comfort and encourage Julie when her husband, Billy Bigelow, the male lead, falls on his knife and dies after a failed robbery attempt.

In the final scene of ***Carousel***, in the commencement ceremony, Louise (Billy and Julie's daughter) remains quiet and sad even when the audience was singing the song. The now invisible Billy was granted a chance to return to earth for this one special day in order to redeem himself and silently motivated his daughter the unhappy Louise to join in the song.

This song inspire so much emotions that it is sung almost everywhere - in concerts, Emmy Awards nights, anniversaries and of course in association football clubs like Liverpool, Dortmund, Celtics, FC Twente, Feyenoord, SC Canbuur, Club Brugge and so forth.

*Here's the lyrics of **You'll Never Walk Alone:***

When you walk through a storm
Hold your head up high
And don't be afraid of the dark.
At the end of a storm
There's a golden sky
And the sweet silver song of a lark.
Walk on through the wind
Walk on through the rain
Though your dreams be tossed and blown.
Walk on, walk on
With hope in your heart
And you'll never walk alone.
You'll never walk alone.
Walk on, walk on
With hope in your heart
And you'll never walk alone
You'll never walk alone.

Your loved ones who have gone to heaven are whispering in your heart encouraging you to PRESS ON to fight until the war is won.

The best rendition, in my view, is by Gerry and the Pacemakers YouTube video:

Gerry & the Pacemaker - You'll Never Walk Alone (Official video)

Here are ***the ten ways to enjoy the journey*** in such a messy world - by correcting the ten errors in our systems and attitudes:

- **US & China rivalry.** India and China signed an agreement of peaceful coexistence by both countries adhering to the principles of self-determination and non-interference. US and China can similarly coexist peacefully by adhering to these principles. However, the military budget of the United States is four times that of China. The US foreign policy is basically one of violent intervention of foreign governments that are hostile to American interests. It is a foreign policy of regime change. China on the other hand pursues a foreign policy of economic development and its funding. After 2013, China's foreign policy takes the form of the Belt and Road Initiative first announced in 2013 in Kazakhstan and later in Indonesia.

- **Origins of evil.** Good means growing out of self-centeredness. Good means the capacity to empathize with other people, to feel compassion for others, and to put their needs at par with our own needs. Good means benevolence, altruism, and sacrifice for the sake of a greater cause. Evil is the inability to empathize with other people. Evil means your own needs are of the utmost importance. Evil is viewing other people as of value only when they can satisfy all your needs and desires.

- **Disunited people.** The top 1% of the world own most of the power, wealth, and privilege while the middle class and the poor struggle daily to make ends meet. The 7 billion people should have power, but in truth had none because they are disunited. What does it take for the masses to be united as one to make the world a better place for all. Can two walk together unless they share the same vision, the same passion, the same objectives, and the same thinking?

- **Corruption.** Corruption is a form of dishonest or unethical conduct by a person entrusted with a position of authority. Corruption takes the form of bribery, kickbacks, and embezzlement. Corruption can occur anywhere - in government, public sector, commerce, politics, police, military, health care, religion, labor unions, science, schools, universities, philosophy, accountancy, banking, investing, and even in the legal system. Scientists, professors, and media can all collude to con the gullible public with fake news and fraudulent endorsements.

- **Warmongers.** Warmongers are greedy and self-righteous people who use war to solve international problems. Such self-righteous people are filled with self-radicalized ideas such as racism and superiority complex. They use force and violence to try to change others , fully ignorant of the fact that it is their intolerance of others that make others retaliate with hostility.

- **Predatory capitalism.** Corruption has made our national and international financial system fraught with dangers for the genuine investors. It is the corruption of national leaders upstream that allows the financial system to be hazardous to retail investors. Even the endowment and pension funds of Harvard and labor unions had been cheated to the tune of billions of dollars each year. All the big players like JP Morgan, Goldman Sachs, Citigroup and central banks are guilty of using sophisticated methods like quantitative easing and repo transactions to manipulate the markets, enriching the 1% of the population.

- **Religious fraud**. Of all the ways scammers can steal your money, experts agree that the most difficult fraud to combat are the ones that turn your own faith against you. Such frauds are called affinity frauds, and they happen most frequently in places of religious worship. Ponzi schemes flourish in religion. Many religious leaders preach faith but their hidden agenda is to accumulate wealth and power.

- **The fake science of psychiatry.** David Rosenhan, professor of psychology at Stanford University conducted an experiment to determine the validity of psychiatric diagnosis. Participants in this experiment feigned hallucinations at several psychiatric hospitals and were duly admitted. They were diagnosed with all forms of psychiatric disorders and were given anti-psychiatric drugs. When these pseudopatients told the hospital staff that they no longer experience hallucinations, they were ignored and had to stay on the average of two weeks. An offended psychiatric hospital administration upon discovering that this was a university experiments, challenged Dr. Rosenhan to send pseudopatients to its facility and it could easily identify them as pseudopatients. Rosenhan agreed. After several weeks, this psychiatric hospital reported to Rosenhan that out of the 250 new patients admitted, its staff could identify 41 of them. Rosenhan informed the hospital that he did not send any pseudopatient to the hospital.

- **Medical fraud.** Corporations rule the world. Pharmaceutical companies - big pharma in short - rule the field of health care, the food industry, and agriculture. This situation is ten times worse in the United States than in Canada and many other countries around the world. Wholesome foods contain bio-active compounds that are just as effective as dangerous drugs prescribed by doctors but without the side effects, and they cost ten times less. To be fair, the medical establishment cannot take the full blame. Most people are plainly not disciplined enough to adhere to the discipline of preventive health care. So when medical issues arise, the doctors and hospital are ready to provide the quick fixes - like medication, radiation, surgery, and physiotherapy.

- **Cyber insecurity.** In 2013, Edward Snowden, a 29-year-old American intelligence expert shocked the world when he revealed that the US government was secretly building a global mass surveillance system to collect every single phone call, text message, and email everywhere in the world. He was involved in building this system, which was capable of prying into the private lives of every person on earth. The data of our private lives were collected and stored on file, ready to be accessed by the US government not only now but potentially forever. Snowden felt that the US government had crossed the red line for him, and he decided to expose the truth at the risk of his liberty and even his life.

Chapter 1

US AND CHINA RIVALRY

The United States and China have the two largest economies. They are usually the largest trading partners of all the other countries. So how their relations pans out will affect every other nation.

Decisions made by China and the US will impact your quality of life. For example, the US has interfered with almost every country around the world, especially Afghanistan, Vietnam, Iran, Venezuela, Iraq, Iran, and Cuba.

China also have tremendous impact on many economies around the world. India felt threaten by the China-Pakistan Economic Corridor. To be fair, both the US and China have their own reasons for their decisions. But the fact still remains that the US-China 21st century war on many fronts will impact all of us.

In his book, ***Stealth War**: how China took over while America's elite slept*, retired US General Robert Spalding gives the shocking news that China has been quietly waging war with the US for many years on many fronts and winning.

The rise of the US

During the second half of the 19th century, more than 30 million immigrants began to arrive from Europe and Asia. It was also an era of vast and successful social and industrial revolutions. The US entered the 20th century on a wave of prosperity and enterprise. By 1914, the US had surpassed Britain and Germany in the output of coal, iron, and steel.

During World War One, the US played an important part in the defeat of Germany and its allies. Democrat President Woodrow Wilson (1913 - 1921) was a leading figure at the Versailles Conference.

The American economy boomed immediately after World War One ended. But this bubble burst and the stock market crashed in October, 1929. The new Democrat President Franklin D Roosevelt introduced policies known as The New Deal to try and put the country on the road to recovery. Because of World War Two, President Roosevelt was kept in the White House for a fourth term.

The US economy boomed again thanks to another major wave of immigration from Europe. It was during the war economy of World War Two that the US rose as the sole global power to defeat Germany and Japan. When the war ended in 1945, it was the Americans that dominated the design of the world financial system, making the US dollar the sole reserve currency and the secretive introduction of central banking. At that time, it was agreed that it should be backed by gold.

The economic boom in the US continued as factories which were used to produce armaments switched to producing consumer goods such as TV sets, fridges, dishwashers, record-players, and tape-recorders. The US GDP figures went up eight-fold.

Contact China

After World War Two, the Soviet Union under Joseph Stalin was given a share of the spoils of war and a seat in the United Nations Security Council. The Soviet Union helped in stopping Nazi Germany from invading Russia but at great cost. Many Russians believed that in their weakened state, foreign forces may attack Russia.

Nikita Krushchev gradually emerged as the leading Russian leader. He began to dismantle Stalin's policy of suppression. Some economic progress was made in improving living standards in the Soviet Union.

When Leonid Brezhnev took over, the world economy was not rosy and the Soviet Union suffered a period of stagnation and decline. Surprisingly, China was even weaker than the Soviet Union and accepted financial and technical help from the Soviet Union.

Meanwhile, the US, fearing that communism may spread to other countries after World War Two, approved a plan to help in rebuilding Germany and Japan. The northern part of Vietnam was dominated by communists and the US sent troops there, at great cost.

The Vietnam War caused high inflation in the US. To overcome the ballooning war expenses, President Nixon ordered, in 1971, a series of economic measures including freeze in wages and price, surcharges on all imports, and the suspension of the direct international convertibility of the US$ to gold. This is known as the Nixon Shock.

At this time, the US had no diplomatic relations with China, only with Taiwan. Nixon found this situation rather odd that 95% of the China's population was not represented in the

United Nations. Nixon began to discuss with his Secretary of State Henry Kissinger to initiate sending subtle overtures to mainland China hinting on the desire to warm up diplomatic relations.

President Nixon sent Henry Kissinger on several secret diplomatic mission to Beijing where he met with Chinese Premier Zhou Enlai. On July 15, 1971, President Nixon announced that he would visit the People's Republic of China.

The historic Nixon visit to China, occurring from 21 to 28 February, 1972 gave the American public amazing views of China for the first time in over two decades. One of the most memorable images was President Nixon and his wife Pat walking along a portion of the Great Wall of China.

This historic Nixon visit to China had vast implications. It shifted the Cold War balance in US's favor. It diminished the diplomatic position of Taiwan, It also allowed the US to extricate itself from the Vietnam War, with China's help.

At the last day of this historic visit, February 28, 1972, the US signed an important diplomatic document known as the Joint Communique of the United States of America and the People's Republic of China, also known as the ***Shanghai Communique***. Both countries pledged that it was in the interest of all nations, for the United States and China to work towards the normalization of their relations.

In the ***Shanghai Communique***, the US and China also agreed that neither they nor any other power should seek hegemony in the Asia-Pacific region. It also acknowledged the One-China policy regarding Taiwan. It signaled the start of a rocky relations but allowed China to grow its economy.

Mao Zidong died in 1976 and there was a power struggle between the communist hard-liners led by the "gang of four" and the reformers. Fortunately for China, Deng Xiaoping, the reformer, was elected as supreme leader in 1978.

Under Deng, the Chinese economy grew but not fast enough. This led to labor union and university student protests. When they turned violent in 1987, Deng, for fear of a major uprising, ordered in the military and many lives were lost. Still, with the help of the US, China was admitted to the World Trade Organization in 2001.

Stealth war

According to several studies, the US and China benefited the most from globalization. Whether such benefits of globalization trickled down to the masses is debatable.

The US allowed China to place Confucius Institutes in many parts of the US, many of them right on university campuses in the US. China also offered enormous sums of money to American experts to create investment funds that funnel funds and technology into the Chinese economy. According to the retired Air Force Brigadier General Robert Spalding, China has succeeded in winning a stealth war while the American elite slept.

This explains why both the US and China had each accumulated debt exceeding $20 trillion over the years. This also explained why China is dominating 5G networks. These 5G networks operate at a 100 times faster rate than the current wireless services which will eventually help support self-driving cars, smart appliances and surgical robots.

In his book, ***Stealth War***, Spalding explains why China must not be allowed to dominate the 5G networks. China's Huawei and fellow Chinese gear maker ZTE Corp have already outcompeted other network providers. Eventually, alternatives to Huawei don't exist because other suppliers won't be able to compete because quotes from Huawei are at least 25% lower.

President Trump took heed of Spalding's warning and banned Huawei from US markets. Huawei's chief financial officer was arrested in Canada, in December 2018 on charges of violating sanctions against Iran. The Trump administration also accused Huawei of spying on behalf of China.

Military rivalry

The Lowy Institute Asia Power Index is an analytical tool that tracks changes in the distribution of power. The Index ranks 25 countries and territories in terms of what military power they have and what they do with what they have. The significant military powers covered are the US, China, Russia, India, Pakistan, Japan, North Korea, South Korea, Australia, and New Zealand.

The 2019 edition has expanded to 126 indicators and evaluate eight thematic measures - military capability and defense networks, economic resources and relationships, diplomatic and cultural influence as well as resilience and future resources.

This Lowy Institute research reveals trends:

- China is fast catching up with the US. This means that neither power is able to exert undisputed primacy in Asia.
- Even if the US decided to decouple from China, both the US and China will always be involved in globalization. Unlike the last cold war, the pushback from other countries against both the US and China will be issue-specific and not ideological.
- Far from being helpless victims, middle powers will become more important during the US-China 21st century war.

When the US and China are gridlocked in a specific issue, the actions of their strongest allies will constitute a marginal advantage.

- This means that countries such as Russia, Iran, Turkey, Germany, France, UK, Italy, Brazil, Saudi Arabia, Japan and India will determine power balance in various regions of the world.

In 2005, the US Department of Defense issued a report ***Energy Futures in Asia***. It used the term "***String of Pearls***" to describe the network of Chinese military and commercial facilities and relationships along the sea lines of communication, extending from the Chinese mainland, through the Straits of Malacca, encircling India, and reaching Port Sudan in the Horn of Africa. It is a geopolitical theory on potential Chinese intentions in the Indian Ocean region.

This geopolitical theory is enhanced by China's Belt and Road Initiative, which is Beijing's trillion-dollar mega-plan similar to the US's Marshall Plan. China's Belt and Road Initiative is practically China's foreign policy.

China desires to strengthen trade links with western Europe, and Africa. Its Belt and Road Initiative is its 21st century silk road. On 1st January, 2017, the first direct freight train left the Chinese city of Yiwu, traveling 12,000 kilometers (7,500 miles) through mountains, deserts, many cultures, through Kazakhstan, Russia, Belarus, Belgium, Germany, Poland, and France.

This freight train, carrying Chinese goods, arrived at a freight depot in Barking, England on 18 January, 2017, a journey of 18 days. On 10 April, 2017, this same freight train departed England for China, carrying European goods such as whiskey, baby milk, and machinery.

Of big concern to the US, India, and many other countries is

China's agreement signed with Pakistan. Pakistan has a population of 213 million people. It has a land area of 881,913 sq.km. It's GDP is around $1.2 trillion, It has the world's 6th largest standing armed forces. Pakistan is the only country in the world that was created in the name of Islam. It is also a nuclear-weapons state. Pakistan has a coastline 1046 kilometers long (650 miles) along the Arabian Sea and the Gulf of Oman off Africa.

China signed an agreement with Pakistan on 22 May 2013. It is known as China-Pakistan Economic Corridor (CPEC). It comprises a collection of infrastructure and energy projects throughout Pakistan. CPEC includes highways that link China's Xinjiang through Khyber Pass to Gwadar Port, thus allowing Chinese goods to be transported over land through Gwadar Port on the way to Africa and West Asia.

CPEC is funded by concessionary loans from China Development Bank, Asian Infrastructure Investment Bank, Silk Road Fund, Exim Bank of China, and Industrial and Commercial Bank of China..

The initial estimated worth of projects is around $46 billion. It is equivalent to all the foreign direct investment in Pakistan since 1970. CPEC will create 2.3 million jobs in Pakistan.

African nations had experienced their exploitation by many European powers. But now, Chinese-initiated megaprojects are sprouting all over Africa. Kenya got its Chinese-built high-speed railway from Nairobi to Mombasa on January, 2017. It is 300 miles long.

But the most amazing mega-project is the Italian-Chinese project at Lake Chad.

Transaqua is an idea developed by the Italian engineering firm Bonfica Spa in the 1970s. It proposed to build a canal, 2,400 kilometers long, from the southern region of the Democratic Republic of Congo, carrying up to 100 billion cubic meters of water per year from the Congo River to Lake Chad which was dried up because of prolonged drought.

Social unrest had erupted because of the drying up of Lake Chad. There was mass migration out of the country. Boko Haram exploited this situation by recruiting terrorists. Even though the proposed Transaqua offered a solution to these problems, western nations and institutions rejected it.

But China came to the rescue. On June 8, 2017, Bonfica Spa signed the historic Italian-Chinese agreement on Lake Chad and ChinaPower, one of China's biggest infrastructure construction company, in the presence of their respective national officials in Hangzhou, China.

In 2016, when Greece was experiencing economic hardship, China's shipping firm Cosco purchased at 600 million euros a majority stake of Piraeus Port, in the Saronic Gulf, Greece's largest harbor. China intends to transform Greece's Piraeus Port into the biggest harbor in Europe.

On March 23, 2019, trade agreements, worth 2.5 billion euros, were signed at Villa Madama in Rome Italy in the presence of Italian Prime Minister Giuseppe Conte and Chinese President Xi Jinping.

So in terms of global influence, China is racing ahead of the US.

Treasure your vote

Elections results in the US, Taiwan, Hong Kong, and several other places will determine whether we'll have more or less stability and prosperity. There is no elections in China because the Chinese Communist Party had approved that Xi Jinping can rule China as long as he chooses to.

Year 2020 is a crucial year for Americans. They will be choosing the next president of the US. Here are the brief profiles of some of the candidates running for the US presidential elections.

President Trump had described the American economy as the best the Americans ever had, which many had disputed. Trump signed the Tax Cuts and Job Acts of 2017, which cut corporate tax rate down to 21%. Trump lowered personal income tax brackets, increased child tax credit, doubled the estate tax exemption to $11.2 million and limited the state and local tax deduction to $10,000

Trump favored bi-lateral trade deals over multi-lateral deals. Trump was in conflict with China over trade deficit, and was critical of TPP and NAFTA. Trump had made large budget cuts to programs regarding renewable energy because he rejected the scientific consensus on climate change.

Trump seeks to trim down federal regulations as well as the size of government. He wants to limit immigration, and was tough on Iran having nuclear power. He is open to negotiation with North Korea to denuclearize the Korean Peninsula.

Trump seems to side with Israel slightly more than Palestinians. So his Israel-Palestinians peace plan is not acceptable to most Middle East countries.

Trump is the subject of an impeachment inquiry and he is prepared to defend his case before Congress. However, the Senate, dominated by the Republicans may vote along party line and acquit President Trump.

In July 6, 2017, President Trump made a speech in Warsaw, Poland to commemorate the Warsaw Uprising in 1944 during World War Two. Some of his remarks were as follows:

We've come to your nation to deliver a very important message. America loves Poland, and America loves the Polish people. The Poles have not only greatly enriched this region, but Polish-Americans have also greatly enriched the United States, and I was truly proud to have their support in the 2016 election. It is a profound honor to stand in this city, by this monument to the Warsaw Uprising, and to address the Polish nation that so many generations have dreamed of a Poland that is safe, strong, and free...

The fundamental question of our time is whether the West has the will to survive. Do we have the confidence in our values to defend them at any cost? Do we have enough respect for our citizens to protect our borders? Do we have the desire and the courage to preserve our civilization in the face of those who would subvert and destroy it.

The Democrats led by Joe Biden, Bernie Sanders, and Elizabeth Warren, plan to reshape corporate America, introduce wealth tax, remove fossil fuel industry from the economy, and launch environment-friendly policies.

Bernie Sanders unveil a $180 billion Green New Deal where solar panels will be installed for public housing. The Democrats will revive regenerative agriculture and support the implementation of the Paris Agreement on climate change. He plans to eradicate the fossil fuel industry and replace it with green energy infrastructure.

US presidential hopeful Andrew Yang proposes a universal basic income plan for every American citizen above the age of 18 to receive a monthly $1000. This is a most powerful way to cure the ills of a predatory capitalism and neoliberalism.

Every presidential candidate looks great when viewed from his or her own public relations campaign documentaries. The fear is that many Americans are so jaded by the political mess that they may not come out to vote.

However, with the recent violent protests against autocratic rulers by millennials in Hong Kong, Taiwan, and Iran and, millennials in America may make up their mind and come forward to vote for their favorite presidential candidate. Only then will be know what the future holds for the US.

Tulsi Gabbard - national unity

In my opinion, a nation that has two dominant political parties suffers from schizophrenia. So we must support any leader who wants to make a brave attempt to cure this disease and achieve NATIONAL UNITY where the government has at least 70% mandate to govern.

So far, the world sees a divided nation, confused about the need for a common ground of principles and freedom from vested interests

To achieve a 70% majority, you cannot be narrow-minded and sectarian. You have to govern by the gold standard of governance. You have to be centered in principles such as meritocracy, pragmatism, integrity, and community over self. You have to protect the rights of minorities.

According to certain observers, the media in the US seems to arbitrarily reduce their coverage of Tulsi Gabbard and Andrew Yang. Whatever their reasons, it is not fair to decide for the American people.

That's why I feel it is fair to air the views of Tulsi Gabbard. Gabbard seems to be the only politician who can really make the United States great again, not by military power but by earning a majority consensus from the people.

US presidential hopeful US Representative from Hawaii, Tulsi Gabbard opposes 'regime change wars' in Syria, Venezuela, and Iran, but is not anti-war. Gabbard believes that such violent intervention only strengthen the terrorists in the Middle East. She highlights the fact that the US government lied to the American people in order to launch the Iraq War. The US military should be used to fight terrorists and not for regime change.

Tulsi Gabbard calls for an end to US involvement in Afghanistan. Gabbard calls for a big reduction of military spending by bringing US troops home.

Gabbard knows the very high costs of unnecessary war. She has first-hand experience because she is a major and had served in Iraq for many years. She hails from Hawaii where people of all races and religious convictions live in harmony. If Hawaii can do it, why not mainland USA?

Gabbard suggested that we can make a move towards NATIONAL UNITY in Washington and throughout the nation with simple acts of ***Aloha***.

Aloha means more than hello and goodbye. The real meaning of ***Aloha*** is:

"I come to you with respect. I come to you with an open heart and with care and compassion."

We are all connected regardless of race or religion. Gabbard asked her mother to prepare 434 boxes of her special macadamia nut toffee for all of her colleagues of both parties. Her mother prepared these boxes, and then made an additional 434 boxes for the staffs of her colleagues.

Gabbard said:

"The very small and simple gestures of reaching out, of saying Aloha helped me begin to build relationships with members on both sides of the aisle. Dealing in a bipartisan way with the myriad of issues facing the nation starts at the top. It starts with leadership.

But it also needs to happen within our communities. It cannot be a one-sided thing that's dictated from the top. We, the people, need to recognize the role that we need to play, whether it's within our workplace, at school, even at home.

Where it must begin is with the recognition that the things that make us angry and frustrated are things that should drive us to bridge this divide, that we have to start at a place of respect. And this is the kind of leadership I would bring.

It's the kind of work that has allowed me to be effective through out my time in Congress. I learned the value of cooperation and finding practical solutions to problems not only in my upbringing, but also during my service in the US army.

I take issue with the Democratic National Committee's handling of the debate process. Regardless, the debate is not the only way to reach the voters. I will speak directly to the American people.

I'll quote from Martin Luther King Jr (1929 - 1968) who said:

Hate begets hate; violence begets violence; toughness beget a greater toughness. We must meet the forces of hate with the power of love...Our aim must never be to defeat or humiliate the white man, but to win his friendship and understanding.

The ultimate weakness of violence is that it is a descending spiral begetting the very thing it seeks to destroy, instead of diminishing evil, it multiplies it. Through violence you may murder the liar, but you cannot murder the lie, nor establish the truth. Through violence you may murder the hater, but you cannot murder hate. In fact, violence merely increases hate.

Returning violence for violence multiplies violence, adding deeper darkness to a night already devoid of stars.

Darkness cannot drive out darkness; only light can do that. Hate cannot drive out hate; only love can do that."

Make your nation and your family great again!

Treasure your vote and vote wisely.

President Jokowi of Indonesia

In October, 2019, newly elected president of Indonesia set a great example to other national leaders with sectarian sentiments. Indonesian President Joko Widodo, also known as Jokowi appointed Prabowo Subianto, opposition leader, as Jokowi's Defence Minister. This gives the ruling party a 90% majority, which I believe is good for the country.

Since Indonesia had a multi-party election system in 1999, no political party had an absolute majority. Therefore, just like in the US, getting things done in the country is like Royal Rumble. A schizophrenic nation is like a family where husband and wife always quarrel over the most trivial things.

As I suggested, a nation that has two dominant parties suffers from schizophrenia. Corruption and sectarianism make people juvenile in their thinking. Living in big houses and driving awesome cars do not make them less juvenile at the world stage.

Based, on that, President Jokowi has made a wise decision, to rope in the support of his opposition for the sake of national unity. National interest must take precedence over minor issues.

This decision is especially wise and timely because the Indonesian capital Jakarta is plagued with pollution, traffic jams and rising sea levels. Jakarta is sinking.

President Jokowi has decided to move its capital to East Kalimantan, which is underdeveloped. This is killing two birds with one stone - to develop Kalimantan and at the same time decentralize Indonesia from Jakarta. This will allow Jakarta to solves its many problems. Jakarta is situated in Java which holds half of Indonesia's population.

Indonesia is not an easy country to govern. President Jokowi believes that when there's a will, there will be a way. As Nelson Mandela said, "Everything seems impossible until it is done."

It is just a matter of doing it and correcting course along the way.

Indonesia is the largest island country in the world. It has 17,000 islands. It has a land area of 1.9 million sq. km. Its population is 267 million. Indonesia's GDP (nominal) is $1.2 trillion. It's GDP (PPP) is $3.7 trillion. Just like Brazil, Indonesia has abundant natural resources and biodiversity.

It is the most populous Muslim-majority country. Indonesian is the official language. Indonesia has over 700 languages and 300 ethnic groups. Islam is the religion of 87.2% of the population, with 9.9% embracing Christianity.

If President Jokowi can do it, so can another national leader.

So, vote wisely.

Peaceful coexistence

The aim of this book is to help you make better decisions. Our forefathers were afflicted with the root of all evils - socio-centrism. Socio-centrism is the belief that one's own race, country and religion is superior to others.

War after war were fought. Do we have enough of that?

After the two world wars, 50 nations signed into force the establishment of the United Nations.

The Charter of the United Nations reads as follows:

We the People of the United Nations,

Determined to save succeeding generations from the scourge of war, which twice in our lifetime has brought untold sorrow to mankind and

To affirm faith in fundamental human rights, in the dignity and worth of the human person, in the equal rights of men and women and of nations large and small, and

To establish conditions under which justice and respect for the obligations arising from treaties and other sources of international law can be maintained, and

To promote social progress and better standards of life in larger freedom,
and to these ends,

To practise tolerance and live together in peace and security, and,

To unite our strength to maintain international peace and security, and

To ensure, by acceptance of principles and the institution of methods, that armed force should not be used, save in the common interest, and

To employ international machinery for the promotion of the economic and social advancement of all peoples,

Have resolved to combine our efforts to accomplish these aims.

Accordingly, our respective Governments, through representatives assembled in the city of San Francisco, who have exhibited their full powers found in good and due form, have agreed to the present Charter of the United Nations and do hereby establish an international organization to be known as the United Nations,

(Signed by 50 nations of the world)

The United Nations has four purposes:

- To preserve world peace and security
- To encourage nations to be just in their actions toward each

other

- To help nations cooperate in trying to solve problems
- To serve as an agency through which nations can work toward these goals.

The United Nations operates under seven principles:

- All member states have equal rights.
- All members are expected to carry out their duties under the Charter.
- They agree to the principles of settling their disputes peacefully.
- They agree not to use force or the threat of force against other nations except in self-defence.
- They agree to help the United Nations in every action it takes to carry out the purposes of the Charter.
- The United Nations agrees to act on the principles that non-member states have the same duties as member states to preserve world peace and security.
- The United Nations accepts the principle of not interfering in the actions of a member nation within its own borders. But these actions must not hurt other nations.

Six major organs were set up to deal with the full spectrum of global issues:

- The General Assembly
- The Security Council
- The Secretariat
- The Economic and Social Council

- The International Court of Justice
- The Trustee Council

The task of keeping world peace was assigned to the Security Council. The UN Security Council is authorized to impose trade sanctions or launch military intervention. It shall have 15 member states, with five member states that will be permanent members, namely, the United States, Russia, Britain, France, and China.

On April 29, 1954, China and India signed the Panchsheel Treaty in Beijing. It spelled out the five principles of peaceful coexistence:

- Mutual respect for each other's territorial integrity and sovereignty.
- Mutual non-aggression.
- Mutual non-interference in each other's internal affairs.
- Equality and cooperation for mutual benefit.
- Peaceful coexistence.

China continues to make reference to these five principles of peaceful coexistence as a major pillar of its foreign policy. Chinese President Xi Jinping will always affirm its commitment to these principles whenever he meet international leaders, especially when launching Belt and Road projects in Africa, Asia, and other parts of the world.

At the personal level

If you want to enjoy the journey, you need to embrace the principles of peaceful coexistence - mutual respect, self-determination, and non-interference with fellow travelers.

This agreement of peaceful coexistence signed by China and India in 1954, can be applied in the relationship between two persons.

We need to respect other people's opinions and choices. Who are we to judge others? We have no such authority over other human beings.

Men are created equal, endowed with the unalienable rights to life, liberty, and the pursuit of happiness.

We have no right to say, for example, that one way of life is superior to another. Here are the many ways of life that we must allow others to choose:

- Pursuing any profession
- Voluntary simplicity
- Country living
- Living off the grid
- Living in a boat-house
- Climbing the corporate ladder
- Refusing a promotion
- Joining the military
- Joining a non-government organization
- Joining the civil service
- Entering politics
- Migrating to another country

Act now on your beliefs

If the US and China want to be great again, they must learn to coexist peacefully, respecting the idea of self-determination and non-interference.

So vote wisely. Vote for a candidate who can achieve a 70% majority to end your country's schizophrenia.

If you want to enjoy the journey, you need to embrace the principles of peaceful coexistence - mutual respect, self-determination, and non-interference.

Decisions have the power to steer and change your life forever. Therefore, nothing affects the quality of your life than your ability to make the right decisions. All that you have achieved or failed to achieved can be traced back to the decisions you've made - on issues concerning your vote, health, wealth, relationships, and life purpose.

Change your beliefs, and you will change your principles, values, virtues, habits, attitudes, social skills, ethics, behavior and so forth.

In life there are no mistakes, only lessons. The secret to resilience, happiness and a less stressful success is to avoid focusing on stagnant traits. Instead, focus on adopting an active, growth-oriented and problem-solving approach to life, and enjoying the journey together with your loved ones.

Here are the beliefs of greatness that will empower you to enjoy the journey with your loved ones:

- That which is hateful to you, do not do to your fellow human beings. Any interpretation of scriptures that bred hatred or disdain for others - whatever their beliefs - is illegitimate. (Hillel)
- True religion is protecting the powerless - orphans, widows, homeless, migrant workers, disabled, and injured soldiers returning from an unnecessary war.

- Power without love is reckless and abusive. Love without power is sentimental and anemic. Power at its best is love implementing the demands of justice. Justice at its best is power correcting everything that stands against love. (Martin Luther King)

- That which matter most must never be at the mercy of things that matter least. (Goethe)

- Courage is not the absence of fear but rather the judgment that something is more important than fear. The brave may not live forever. But the cautious do not live at all. (Meg Cabot)

- So long as you open your heart to beauty, hope, cheer, courage and power, so long are you young. (Samuel Ulman). I know of no more encouraging fact than the unquestionable ability of man to elevate his life by conscious endeavor (Henry David Thoreau).

- We should encourage each other to follow the rules of considerate conduct such as think before we act, listen more, argue less, seek first to understand, think twice before asking favors, avoid shifting responsibility and blame, avoid jumping to conclusions, respect other's opinion, and enjoying the journey with your loved ones.

- If you want to achieve what you've never achieved before, you have to grow to become what you've never become before. (Brian Tracy). Insanity is doing the same over and over again and expecting different results. No problem can be solved at the same level of consciousness that created it. (Albert Einstein)

- Success and cheerfulness in life are not the result of what we have but rather how we live. What we do with the things we already have now makes the biggest difference in the quality of our life. (Tony Robbins)

- Studies have shown that companies hire for attitude and train for skills. (Singapore Airlines).
- Humility is the beginning of wisdom. (Zen habits)
- A foolish definition of success is the attainment of a certain amount of money, power, and privilege. A wise definition of success is enjoying the journey of lifelong learning with your loved ones.
- All men are created equal, endowed with the unalienable rights to life, liberty and the pursuit of happiness. (US Declaration of Independence)
- The world will be safer and prosperous when all nations adhere to the principles of peaceful coexistence where there is mutual respect for each other's territorial sovereignty and the right to self-determination and non-interference. (China-India)
- Whether a cat is black or white makes no difference. A cat that catches mice is a good cat. Whether we label an ideology socialism, capitalism, communism, or authoritarianism makes no difference. A government that can provide affordable subsidized public housing, meaningful jobs, efficient transport system, clean environment, fantastic schools, universal health care, recreation centers, and national security is a good government and should be given a strong mandate to govern. (Deng Xiaoping)
- Every nation must strive to avoid contracting the national disease of schizophrenia where there are two equally dominant sectarian political parties, bickering with each other like two juveniles. It is best if there is a political party that promote universal values that protect the rights of minorities so as to gain at least 70% of popular vote thus attaining a strong mandate to govern.

- Workers must enjoy democracy at the workplace where they have a say in the management of the company and reserve the right to buy the company if the owners decide to sell.
- All citizens must have a fair share in the prosperity of the nation. This can be achieved by practicing universal basic income (UBI) calculated as a small percentage of the living wage. UBI is able to soften the ills of neoliberalism by reducing the pain and frustration of the underprivileged who are the victims of the wealth gap between the rich and the poor. UBI is able to reduce the risk of violent civil unrest.
- Every citizen must be given universal healthcare.
- Every person has the right to demand privacy, especially when he or she has not committed any crime. (Edward Snowden)
- Every person has the right to choose his own way of life without being judged or criticized so long as he or she respects the rule of law. He can choose voluntary simplicity, country living, living off the grid, any profession, urban competition, climbing the corporate ladder, activism, the military, or politics.
- Whistleblowers should be protected by law when they expose the wrongdoings within the company or government.

Chapter 2

ORIGINS OF EVIL

Good means growing out of self-centeredness. Good means the capacity to empathize with other people, to feel compassion for others, and to put their needs at par with our own needs. Good means benevolence, altruism, and sacrifice for the sake of a greater cause.

Evil is the inability to empathize with other people. Evil means your own needs are of the utmost importance. Evil is viewing other people as of value only when they can satisfy all your needs and desires.

Nevertheless, it is dangerous to allow the justice system of any country to define what is good and what is evil.

Many justice systems, in good conscience, are founded on existing discriminatory beliefs. There are criminals in all sectors and industries. People who know how to work the system such as hiring the best lawyers can get away with crime whereas the unkempt and jobless look guilty.

Human nature is complex. In most cases, there are extenuating circumstances that can strongly influence a person's behavior. While our assessment may be accurate, it is in sentencing that we must be more merciful. Restorative justice is superior to punitive justice.

Power without love is reckless and abusive. Love without power is sentimental and anemic. Power at its best is love implementing the demands of justice. Justice at its best is power correcting everything that stands against love. These were the thoughts of Martin Luther King.

Studies have shown that power corrupts, and absolute power corrupts absolutely. It follows therefore that we must be careful who we bestow power to.

From power comes the opportunity to instill fear and get away with it. We seem to know what good or evil is - in theory. In reality, other elements especially fear and rage will come to disrupt our usual behavior.

Rage

In 1837, in a small Austrian village, an unmarried 42-year-old peasant woman named Maria Anna Schickgruber gave birth to a baby boy. She named her son Alois. When Alois was five years old, his mother married a millworker surnamed Hiedler.

In 1847, Maria died. Hiedler left Alois in the care of his brother Johann Nepomunk Hiedler, and took off. Alois grew up and, to his uncle's immense pride, became an official customs agent. Somehow the name on official records was misspelled as Hitler.

Alois Hitler was a womanizer. He had an illegitimate daughter. He then married a sickly woman. He thoughtfully hired two young attractive maids to help around the house - Franziska Mitzelberger and his own 16-year-old cousin Klara Polzl.

Alois became involved with both girls and his wife divorced him. Franziska died of tuberculosis and Polzi became his mistress. The couple had three children who died in infancy. A son was born in 1889 and they named him Adolfus.

Alois was very strict with his son Adolfus. Alois would regularly give Adolfus a sound thrashing. In contrast, Adolfus's mother Klara doted on him. In 1903, Alois died of pleural hemorrhage when Adolfus was 14 years old.

Klara left Adolfus to pursue his dream of becoming an artist. Even though Adolfus hated his father, he adopted his father's uncontrollable fits of rage. He also became a womanizer, employing his half-niece as his maid and had an intimate relationship with her.

In 1907, Adolfus Hitler lost his beloved mother to breast cancer. He was terribly distressed. He moved to Germany in 1913 to join the military. He was very eloquent and decided to join the German Workers' Party (DAP) in 1919. Hitler rose to become leader of DAP in 1921 which was later renamed NSAP.

In1923, Hitler attempted to seize power in Munich but failed. He was imprisoned. In jail, he dictated the first volume of his autobiography and political manifesto ***Mein Kampf*** *(My Struggle)*.

When Hitler was release from prison in 1924, he worked the system to gain popular support. He attacked the Treaty of Versailles and promoted Pan-Germanism, anti-semitism, and anti-communism with his tremendous charismatic oratory. He twisted this theory into explaining that all the hateful things came from a Jewish conspiracy.

Hitler rose to power as Chancellor of Germany, riding on the hatred the Germans had for victors of World War One, namely Britain and France, Hitler abrogated the restrictions imposed on his country and turned the Weimar Republic into Nazi Germany.

Hitler started manufacturing armaments and invaded Poland on September 1, 1939. Britain and France declared war on Germany. Millions of non-Germans were rounded up to support the war industries. The weak and the sick were killed. At the end of World War Two when Germany surrendered to the Allies, 5.5 million Jews and 19.3 million civilians and prisoners of war died.

Foolish definition of success.

Hitler succeeded in becoming the leader of a political party. Hitler succeeded in becoming the Chancellor of Germany. Hitler succeeded in invading Poland. Hitler succeeded in killing Jews.

Is this the kind of success you want?

Good means growing out of self-centeredness. Good means the capacity to empathize with other people, to feel compassion for others, and to put their needs at par with our own needs. Good means benevolence, altruism, and sacrifice for the sake of a greater cause.

Evil is the inability to empathize with other people. Evil means your own needs are of the utmost importance. Evil is viewing other people as of value only when they can satisfy all your needs and desires.

Foolish people focus on the wrong things. Reflect on this Buddhist wisdom - money can't buy everything:

Money can buy a house but not a home.
Money can buy a bed but not sleep.
Money can buy a clock but not time.
Money can buy a book but not knowledge.
Money can buy food but not appetite.
Money can buy a position but not respect.
Money can buy blood but not life.
Money can buy insurance but not safety.
Money cannot buy everything.

Don't you agree that it is better to eat a simple meal with your loved ones than to feast in a palace full of intrigue and betrayal?

Don't you agree that a cheerful heart work like good medicine but a crushed spirit dries up the bone?

Don't you agree that almost all painful feelings emanates from an unwise way of looking at reality?

Don't you agree that when you erase such erroneous views and bad attitude, suffering ends?

Don't you agree high IQ people do dumb things because of arrogance, isolation, recklessness, and overreaching?

In early April 2014, the Sewol ferry was preparing to set sail from Incheon near Seoul, South Korea. It carried 200 students from Danwon High School. Together with other tourists and a crew of 33, there were a total of 417 people on board the Sewol ferry. They were on the way sailing to Jeju Island.

On 16 April, 2014, before reaching Jeju Island, the Sewol ferry sank and 417 lives were lost. It was South Korea's worst maritime disaster. This tragedy paralyzed South Korean society and began a period of soul-searching.

While the rest of South Korea was preparing to celebrate Liberation Day in August, an estimated 80,000 people crowded Seoul's City Hall. Parents, students, laborers, religious figures, and activists gathered there to demand to know exactly what happened.

Investigations revealed issues that plagued South Korean society. The Cheonghaejin Marine Company was the owner of the Sewol ferry service. The South Korean government habitually gave special treatment to big companies, especially the conglomerates. The Sewol ferry had carried excess cargo 139 times since the start of its service in 2013.

Despite this flouting of cargo regulations, the Sewol ferry regularly passed government safety checks. Government officials had taken bribes and the ferry owners had broken the law.

Investigations revealed that out of the 33 crew members, 19 of them including the captain and the first mate were irregular workers. Such irregular workers were not given proper training. They were paid less than half of full-time workers. Irregular labor was prevalent in South Korea.

It was discovered that when this tragedy happened, the government manipulated the press reports and the public was given false information about the accident. Violent protests led to the resignation of the president of KBS broadcasting service.

The Police issued a warrant of arrest of the boss of Cheonghaejin Marine Company - billionaire businessman Yoo Byung-eun. He was found missing shortly after the disaster, sparking a massive manhunt.

In June, 2014, the Police confirmed, after DNA tests, that a badly decomposed body found in a park belong to Yoo.

Man's search for meaning

In his book, ***Man's Search For Meaning,*** Viktor E Frankl demonstrates that even in the midst of extreme suffering, man still has the freedom to choose - to survive or to give up.

Frankl was one of the millions of non-Germans rounded up and kept in bestial concentration camps. His father, mother, brother, and his wife died in camps or were sent to the gas ovens.

Like all the prisoners of war, Frankl was stripped of every possession. He was always starved, suffering cold and regular brutality. Every hour, he feared a recall for extermination.

In the concentration camps, every circumstance conspired to

make the prisoners lose their mind. All the familiar goals in life were snatched away. What alone remained was the last human freedom - the ability to choose one's attitude in a given set of circumstances

By focusing on why he should continue to hope, Frankl's capacity to rise above his outward fate remained strong. Here is a uniquely human capacity that can be developed into a sense of responsibility to his own life and to its meaning.

Frankl was fond of quoting Nietzsche:

*He who has a **why** to live can bear with almost any **how**.*

A person's will to continue living is strong when he is able to make a larger sense out of his apparently senseless suffering.

Man has a deep desire to search for meaning, to weave these slender threads of a broken life into a firm pattern of meaning and responsibility. When we accept that life is suffering, when we truly see this truth, when we truly understand and accept it, then behold, life is no longer difficult.

In his book, ***The Road Less Traveled,*** Scott Peck reveals a new psychology of love, traditional values and spiritual growth. The ideas he has presented in his book stem from, for the most part, his day-to-day clinical work with patients as they struggle to avoid or to gain ever higher levels of maturity.

Peck makes two assumptions. One is that he made no distinction between the mind and the spirit. This means that there is no distinction between the process of achieving spiritual growth and achieving mental growth.

The second assumption is that this process of spiritual and mental growth is a complex, arduous, and lifelong task. And since it is a long journey, why not enjoy the journey - because there is value in the suffering.

Life is a series of problems. Do we want to moan about them or solve them? Do we want to teach ourselves and our children to solve them?

Discipline is the basic set of tools we require to solve the problems of living. Without discipline we can solve nothing. With only some discipline we can solve only some problems. With total discipline, we can solve all problems.

There are four tools of discipline:

- **Delaying gratification** (meeting pain before pleasure; patience, impulse control, think before you act)
- **Acceptance of responsibility** (control your destiny or someone else will)
- **Dedication to truth** (face reality as it is, not as it was, or as you wish it were)
- **Balancing** (wisdom, emotional intelligence, experience)

These are evidently not complex tools which require extensive training. To the contrary, these are simple tools and almost all children are adept in the use of them by the age of ten. Yet presidents and kings will often forget to use them, to their own downfall.

The will to use these tools is love.

What is love?

Scot Peck defines love as the WILL to extend one's self for the purpose of nurturing one's own or another's spiritual growth.

Self-love and the love of others go hand in hand. That is why when we hate something about ourselves, we tend to hate the same thing in others. When we learn how to take care of ourselves, we have the capacity to take care of others.

What is WILL?

Will is desire of sufficient intensity that translate desire into action. The decision to act is part of will.

Patience as impulse control

In 1954, neuroscientists had identified a part of the brain called the limbic cortex. It has been implicated as the seat of emotion, addiction, mood, and lots of other mental and emotional processes.

The limbic cortex is the primitive part of the human brain. Many people called it the lizard brain. This is the type of brain that lizards have. It is in charge of fight, flight, feeding, fear, freezing up, fornication, breathing, heart beat, and metabolism.

Our lizard brain sits at the top of our spine. It is in command control for the human body. It lurks in our skull and may occasionally cause us to perform primeval actions that actually endangers us or those close to us. If we do not develop other parts of our brain, we will become our own worst enemy.

Impulse control disorders include a number pf mental conditions that may cause social, legal, occupational, and financial mistakes. Such disorders include gambling, stealing, setting fires, and sexual misconduct.

The strategy that has a highest leverage on taming our natural impulses came from James J Heckman. Governments have consulted him on the importance of early childhood education. In his book, ***Giving Kids A Fair Chance*** - *a strategy that works,* Heckman, a top economist, weighs in on one of the most urgent questions of our times:

What is the source of inequality and what is the remedy?

Heckman reveals that the accident of birth is the greatest source of inequality today. Children born into disadvantage are, by the time they start kindergarten, already at risk of dropping out of school, teen pregnancy, crime, and a lifetime of low-wage work.

Current social and education policies directed toward children focus on improving cognition. But studies have shown that success in life requires more than just a high IQ. Heckman calls for a refocus of social policy toward early childhood interventions designed to enhance both cognitive abilities as well as emotional intelligence.

Studies have shown that the earlier we intervene, the better will be our society. How early must be be? Evidence has shown that the pinnacle of achievement is to invest in the education of girls. Girls' education will strengthen economies and create jobs. Communities become more stable and can recover faster from conflict when girls are educated. Investing in girls' education is good for our planet.

Prison as a reflection of national values

Fyodor Dostoevsky was a Russian author of fictional novels who was exiled for ten years in Siberia for political indiscretion. When he returned to Moscow, he wrote his second novel named ***Crime and Punishment***, published in 1866.

Crime and Punishment focuses on the mental anguish and moral dilemmas of an impoverished ex-student, named Rodion Raskolnikov who lived in St. Petersburg. Raskolnikov planned to kill an unscrupulous pawnbroker and steal her money. Raskolnikov thought that after his misdeed, he could liberate himself from poverty and proceed to do great deeds.

However, once he succeeded in carrying out his plot, he found himself racked with confusion, paranoia, and disgust for what he had done.

On reflection, Fyodor Dostoyevsky wrote:

The degree of civilization in a society can be judged by entering its prisons.

If this is a fair assessment, then prisons in the US would reflect the US as a vindictive and violent nation. The US makes up just 5% of the world's population but incarcerates 25% of the world's prisoners. The US prison guards take a punitive approach to control the inmates.

Shortly after World War II, the victorious Allies, led by the United States launched a plan to rebuild Germany. In 1949, Germany approve a new constitution. Article 1 reads as follows:

Human dignity shall be inviolable. To respect and protect it shall be the duty of all state authorities.

The German prison system follows Article 1 of Germany's Constitution faithfully. Whether a nation is good or evil can be ascertained by visiting its prisons.

In Germany, prison is not punitive. It is designed to mirror normal life as much as possible. The system believes that most of them can be re-integrated into society.

Prison staff are social workers who believe that people can be trained to handle conflict in constructive ways.

A German prison is designed like a college campus, with immaculate facilities for organized sports, video games and communal dining.

Each inmate is given his own cell, measuring 100 sq. feet, with a toilet, a wash basin and one single bed. He has his own key to his cell. Inmates cook their meals in a big kitchen with knifes, cutlery, and cooking utensils.

Inmates who show good behavior are allowed to leave prison for work or weekend getaways.

There is hope yet for the US prison system. A Connecticut

prison is trying out the German-style rehabilitation called TRUE - Truthful, Respectful, Understanding, and Elevating. Inmates here were skeptical about its effectiveness when they first enter the prison. Many of them have since changed their mind, because this TRUE program is working.

Prison systems in other countries are also enjoying success in such an approach to prison rehab. For example, Brazilian inmates can gain early release through the prisons' ***Redemption Through Reading*** scheme.

Prisoners will get four days taken off their sentences for every book they read. Each prisoner is given four weeks to read each book. At the end of it, he or she has to write an essay with correct use of paragraphs, be free of corrections, use proper margins, and legible fluent writing.

The sentence reduction is capped at 48 days, meaning twelve book-essays a year.

Act now on your beliefs

Evil flourish when good people who know do nothing.

The decision to invest in girls' education will have the biggest impact on social progress. Next in impact on society is the decision to invest in early childhood education.

Whether you are parent, grand child, teacher, colleague or friend, you can experience life's greatest joy by bringing out the best in people.

When you believe, they will achieve.

Decisions have the power to steer and change your life forever. Therefore, nothing affects the quality of your life than your ability to make the right decisions. All that you have achieved or failed to achieved can be traced back to the decisions you've made - on issues concerning your vote, health, wealth, relationships, and life purpose.

Change your beliefs, and you will change your principles, values, virtues, habits, attitudes, social skills, ethics, behavior and so forth.

In life there are no mistakes, only lessons. The secret to resilience, happiness and a less stressful success is to avoid focusing on stagnant traits. Instead, focus on adopting an active, growth-oriented and problem-solving approach to life, and enjoying the journey together with your loved ones.

Here are the beliefs of greatness that will empower you to enjoy the journey with your loved ones:

- That which is hateful to you, do not do to your fellow human beings. Any interpretation of scriptures that bred hatred or disdain for others - whatever their beliefs - is illegitimate. (Hillel)
- True religion is protecting the powerless - orphans, widows, homeless, migrant workers, disabled, and injured soldiers returning from an unnecessary war.
- Power without love is reckless and abusive. Love without power is sentimental and anemic. Power at its best is love implementing the demands of justice. Justice at its best is power correcting everything that stands against love. (Martin Luther King)
- That which matter most must never be at the mercy of things that matter least. (Goethe)
- Courage is not the absence of fear but rather the judgment that something is more important than fear. The brave may not live forever. But the cautious do not live at all. (Meg Cabot)
- So long as you open your heart to beauty, hope, cheer,

courage and power, so long are you young. (Samuel Ulman). I know of no more encouraging fact than the unquestionable ability of man to elevate his life by conscious endeavor (Henry David Thoreau).

- We should encourage each other to follow the rules of considerate conduct such as think before we act, listen more, argue less, seek first to understand, think twice before asking favors, avoid shifting responsibility and blame, avoid jumping to conclusions, respect other's opinion, and enjoying the journey with your loved ones.
- If you want to achieve what you've never achieved before, you have to grow to become what you've never become before. (Brian Tracy). Insanity is doing the same over and over again and expecting different results. No problem can be solved at the same level of consciousness that created it. (Albert Einstein)
- Success and cheerfulness in life are not the result of what we have but rather how we live. What we do with the things we already have now makes the biggest difference in the quality of our life. (Tony Robbins)
- Studies have shown that companies hire for attitude and train for skills. (Singapore Airlines).
- Humility is the beginning of wisdom. (Zen habits)
- A foolish definition of success is the attainment of a certain amount of money, power, and privilege. A wise definition of success is enjoying the journey of lifelong learning with your loved ones.
- All men are created equal, endowed with the unalienable rights to life, liberty and the pursuit of happiness. (US Declaration of Independence)
- The world will be safer and prosperous when all nations

adhere to the principles of peaceful coexistence where there is mutual respect for each other's territorial sovereignty and the right to self-determination and non-interference. (China-India)

- Whether a cat is black or white makes no difference. A cat that catches mice is a good cat. Whether we label an ideology socialism, capitalism, communism, or authoritarianism makes no difference. A government that can provide affordable subsidized public housing, meaningful jobs, efficient transport system, clean environment, fantastic schools, universal health care, recreation centers, and national security is a good government and should be given a strong mandate to govern. (Deng Xiaoping)
- Every nation must strive to avoid contracting the national disease of schizophrenia where there are two equally dominant sectarian political parties, bickering with each other like two juveniles. It is best if there is a political party that promote universal values that protect the rights of minorities so as to gain at least 70% of popular vote thus attaining a strong mandate to govern.
- Workers must enjoy democracy at the workplace where they have a say in the management of the company and reserve the right to buy the company if the owners decide to sell.
- All citizens must have a fair share in the prosperity of the nation. This can be achieved by practicing universal basic income (UBI) calculated as a small percentage of the living wage. UBI is able to soften the ills of neoliberalism by reducing the pain and frustration of the underprivileged who are the victims of the wealth gap between the rich and the poor. UBI is able to reduce the risk of violent civil unrest.
- Every citizen must be given universal healthcare.
- Every person has the right to demand privacy, especially

when he or she has not committed any crime. (Edward Snowden)

- Every person has the right to choose his own way of life without being judged or criticized so long as he or she respects the rule of law. He can choose voluntary simplicity, country living, living off the grid, any profession, urban competition, climbing the corporate ladder, activism, the military, or politics.
- Whistleblowers should be protected by law when they expose the wrongdoings within the company or government.

Chapter three

DISUNITED PEOPLE

David Korten was a senior advisor on development management at the Philippines branch of the US Agency for International Development (USAID) for eight years. He experienced first hand the heroic struggles, spiritual grounding, and generosity of people from several parts of Southeast Asia.

David Korten also saw how globalization has seriously disrupted human relationships and community life, causing significant hardship for the very people national development was supposed to benefit. It seems that only the upper class of society was enjoying the fruits of globalization.

Korten saw development's presumed beneficiaries struggling to maintain their dignity and the quality of their lives. They were hurt by the development agencies and projects that were colonizing their resources. The more Korten thought about these things, the more he became alienated from the mainstream developmental thinking.

Korten left USAID but remained in Southeast Asia, keeping in touch with the NGO community concerned with the ills of globalization. Korten synthesized the collective insights and published his book entitled, ***Getting to the 21st Century: Voluntary Action and the Global Agenda.***

Korten and several of his friends founded the ***People-Centered Development Forum (PCDForum).*** It is a global citizen network engaged in articulating and advancing a people-centered vision of the future. It aims to redefine development practice in line with that vision.

When corporations rule the world

In November 1992, Korten traveled to Baguio, a Philippine mountain resort town, to meet with the leaders of several Asian NGOs. They engaged in a ten-day reflection on Asian development experience and its implications for NGO strategies. Behind the glitz of national development, only the rich got richer and the poor poorer. Corporations were invading workers' privacy, providing poor service, paying less than living wages, and disrupting family life.

By the late 1980s, Korten began to comprehend the full dimensions of the unfolding human tragedy. Earlier, he had assumed that such a human tragedy was confined to the Asian countries in which he was most involved. Korten was horrified when similar trends of social and environmental disintegration was happening in the United States, Europe and Japan as well.

Eventually, Korten arrived at the inescapable truth. In the name of creating new wealth, the benefits only accrued to the top 1% of society while the rest of humanity was impoverished.

Through deregulation and the removal of national economic borders, we have created a global economy more powerful than any national government. This global economy is flying on autopilot. The activities of corporations that have disrupted or ruin the lives of workers are as follow:

- The excesses of CEO compensation which is more than 200 times the wages of workers, including bonus that is calculated based on stock prices. So the hidden agenda of CEOs was to jack up stock prices even if it hurts their employees.

- The unceremonious firing of tens of thousands of employees by companies reporting record profits.
- The wholesale movement of previously well-paid jobs to to countries where workers are paid very low wages.
- The wave of buyouts by corporate raiders.

Battle of Seattle

Korten decided to return to New York, break his silence and take to the streets. He decided to write another book to cover these issues. Corporations now rule the world. The rage and frustration were reaching an explosive level. The indigenous people of Chiapas initiated an armed rebellion on January 1, 1994. This event was well-covered by the press.

Korten titled his book ***When Corporations Rule the World*** which got published in 1995. The main theme of his book was that globalization had allowed corporations and financial elites to replace democracy.

Teach-ins sprang up in many parts of the world, boosted by a global movement which had many names - *Fair Trade Movement, Anti-globalization, the Pro-Democracy Movement, and the Living Democracy Movement.*

In 1996, Korten joined Sarah van Gelder to cofound the ***Positive Futures Network***, located in Bainbridge Island, Washington. It is the publisher for the ***YES! A Journal of Positive Futures.*** Activists began to gather strength in numbers, using this magazine and Korten's ***When Corporation Rule the World*** as their bible for the living democracy movement.

The WTO announced that there would be a ministerial conference on November 11, 1999. It was to be convened at the Washington State Convention and Trade Center in Seattle, Washington, USA. It's aim was to launch a new millennial round of trade negotiations.

Activists began planning a massive demonstration. They came from the Anti-globalization movement, Direct Action Network, NGOs, labor unions, students, religious groups, and angry workers. On that day, more than 50,000 jammed the streets around the convention center in Seattle. It was so bad that law enforcement agents were spraying pepper spray at the crowd. But the protesters succeeded in getting the WTO conference canceled.

157 individuals were arrested. But there were later released for lack of sufficient evidence. They got compensation totaling $250,000

The International Monetary Fund (IMF) and World Bank had scheduled to meet in Washington DC on 16 & 17 April, 2000. Again, protesters managed to get this conference canceled. The strength of the argument presented by the protesters was strong. The current form of globalization enriched only the wealthy people of society and transnational corporations while the majority of people remain poor.

Team learning

Peter M Senge is the Director of the System Thinking and Organization Learning Program at the Sloan School of Management, Massachusetts Institute of Technology.

In his book, ***The Fifth Discipline***, Senge reveals that the most successful corporations will be something called the learning organization. The organizations that excel will be those that discover how to tap their people's commitment and capacity to learn at every level in the company.

What will distinguish these companies from the traditional "controlling" organizations will be the mastery of certain basic disciplines. The five competent technologies which provide the vital dimensions in building organizations that can truly learn as a great team are:

- **System thinking** (the invisible fabrics of interrelated actions in business, relationships and other human endeavors)
- **Personal mastery** (emotional intelligence and proficiency)
- **Mental models** (internal representations, state of mind, paradigm, beliefs)
- **Building a shared VISION** (a shared picture of the future that can make your nation and family great again)
- **Team learning** (how to raise the team IQ from below 100 to high IQ by applying principles, values, virtues, and tools such as the Six Thinking Hats)

The Fifth Discipline draws on science, spiritual values, psychology, and the cutting edge of management thought.

To cause a deep change in society and challenge corporate dominance, the living democracy movement must have powerful tools such as Senge's competent technologies in order to form an organized force to fight unbridled power, wealth, and privilege. These principles of creative cooperation can be apply to two best friends, a couple, siblings, a family, a team, and the participants of the living democracy movement.

People must be convinced, committed and united, sharing the vision of a more just economic order. Otherwise, it will not have the force to cause a deep change in society.

Six Thinking Hats

Argument makes us defensive, cutting us from so many alternative narratives that could have helped solve problems of the human race.

Edward de Bono has had faculty appointments at the universities of Oxford, Cambridge, and Harvard. He is widely regarded as the leading authority in the direct teaching of thinking as a skill.

Edward de Bono originated the concept of lateral thinking. He developed formal techniques for deliberate creative thinking. He has written more than 62 books which have been translated into 37 languages. He has made two TV series and there are over 4 million references to his work on the Internet.

Edward de Bono runs the most widely used program for the direct teaching of thinking in schools. The appeal of de Bono's work is its simplicity and practicality.

In his book, ***Six Thinking Hats***, ***Edward de Bono*** commented:

There is nothing more sad and wasteful than a roomful of intelligent and highly paid people waiting for a chance to attack something the speaker has said.

With the Six Hats method, the fullest use is made of everyone's intelligence, experience, and information. The Six Hats also removes all "ego" from the discussion process.

The need for the Six Hats is based on an understanding of how the brain chemicals change with the mode of thinking. Using this method, one major corporation reduced the time taken for multinational project discussions from 30 days to just 2 days.

Argument is inefficient, ineffective, and extremely slow. Argument was never designed to be constructive. The parallel thinking of the Six Hats is rapidly replacing argument around the world. From senior executives at major corporations like Siemens, NTT, Prudential (US) to four-year-olds in school. From Khmer villages in Cambodia to senior government departments.

For 2,400 years we have been content with argument which was never designed to be constructive. Discovering 'what is' may not be the same as designing 'what can be'.

Your thinking is poor and wasteful when your objective is to prove yourself right and other people wrong.

Productivity can be increased many times when the Six Hats method is used. It is based on the simple concept that a thinker should employ one mode of thinking at a time. There are six modes of thinking which alone is deficient but when combined will boost productivity.

The six hats represent six types of thinking. Each hat is given a color that is strongly associated with its direction. Just like ordinary hats, hats can be put on or taken off. Switching one hat for another expands our capacity to think fully on an issue rather than stuck with a narrow point of view. Each type of thinking must be given enough time to blossom.

The value of a hat as a symbol is that it indicates a role when you put it on. So when we say let's put on a particular hat, all of us will think in the same direction instead of the unproductive habit of attacking the speaker:

The white hat

The white hat symbolizes white paper. We take notes, putting information onto paper, information that we need to solve a problem. The white hat is neutral. Information can come from anywhere in the world, from any discipline, regardless of race, language or religion.

For example, there is a difference between cultures. The western notion is that ideas should be hammered into shape by argument. The Japanese, for example, go to a meeting to listen and take note of other people's experience and information.

The red hat

It is not true that emotions spoils thinking. Human beings are emotional creatures. These emotions must be surfaced. When we put on the red hat, we want people to express their true feelings, emotions, and intuition - without any need to explain or to justify them.

Emotions must not be suppressed, because if they are not expressed now, it will come out one way or another later. So we might as well express them now.

The black hat

The black hat is similar to naysaying. We are cautious and careful, and we naturally want to point out what is wrong, what does not fit, and what will not work.

The black hat is always logical and protect us from breaking the law or do silly things. Feelings belong to the red hat. The black hat talks about logical reasons why a thing will or will not work. The black hat points out the weaknesses and risk of failure.

The yellow hat

The yellow hat represents optimism just like sunshine. We look for advantages, benefits and value if we take a certain direction. These attributes should be logically based. The yellow hat is also positive thinking and constructive thinking, with a strong desire to make things happen.

Our brain is wired for survival first. So while we can easily spend hours with the black hat, the yellow hat requires a lot of deliberate encouragement.

The green hat
Vegetation is green. Vegetation is energy, growth, and creation. The green hat is creative thinking, like putting a lift outside the building, or arriving at a building from the top and so forth.

The green hat thinking is also the thinking about possibilities. It denotes new ideas, new concepts, new perceptions, new approaches, alternatives, changes, reform, and innovation.

The blue hat
The blue hat represents the blue sky above. You think of viewing the whole situation from the sky, getting an overview, seeing the big picture.

The blue hat thinking is also like the conductor of an orchestra, seeing that every musical instrument is played well at the right tempo, right volume, and so forth.

The blue hat is also like the ringmaster of a circus, where acrobats, animals, equipments are all doing their part to give a great show.

So the blue hat is for process control. It is usually used at the beginning of a meeting and at the end. At the beginning, we look at the agenda, and at the end, we want to round up the discussion and remind the group what will be the follow up actions to be taken by different people.

Walking hand in hand

Can two walk together unless they agree?

Can two walk together unless they have the same beliefs about greatness?

Can two walk together unless they share the same vision?

Can two walk together unless they share the same principles, values, and virtues?

But you may ask:

What should I do if we seem to be mismatched?

The answer to this question is that there is no perfect match in this world. The mismatch comes from flaws in character and attitude. These are malleable entities and we can all improve ourselves when we are facing grave challenges to our very survival.

In times like this, you need creative cooperation.

You will come closer together when you focus on meaning, responsibility, and the promises you have made to your loved ones and friends. When we make a conscious effort to converge towards the common ground of principles, values, and virtue, we become more matched.

Every human being is unique. So what we need to do is to embark on a journey of lifelong journey of spiritual growth. Remember what Albert Einstein says about insanity. Insanity is doing the same thing over and over again and expecting different results. No problem can be solved in the same level of consciousness that create it.

Mismatch is a source of making excuses.

So if you want to grow, you must allow other people's reasonable ideas to improve you. You become less and less mismatched, and more and more matched. This is life.

So long as you are willing to meet people part way, win-win solutions can be found. When you adopt a wonderful give-and-take attitude, and accept certain trade-offs, things can continually progress. Flexibility, adaptability and reasonableness are keys to getting along with others - so long as you are not self-righteous. Remember - humility is the key to wisdom.

We may have our differences. But if we are willing to base our decisions on results and principles, we can get along just fine.

When we have the same objective of taking our lives back from corporate dominance, when we hate corporations to rule the world, we can team up and fight what we hate, together as an A-Team.

When we have the same enemies to hate such as religious frauds and warmongers, we can be friends forever.

Never give up

As Stephen Covey wisely said:

No family is free from challenges from its own members. Only great habits will give rise to great families. The strength of the nation is built on the integrity of the home.

Still, this journey is a very long and hazardous one.

This is because we live in a world that is volatile, uncertain, complex, dangerous, and high competitive.

The thing that will keep us fighting is our sense of responsibility and meaning. We, the people, when united, can never be defeated.

As the spiritual warfare wages on, what will keep us going is not our talents, it's not our genius, it's not our education, but our strong and firm belief that what we are doing is worth the suffering.

So let us never give up the good fight. We need to persist until the war is won.

Former US president Calvin Coolidge says it best about PERSISTENCE:

Nothing in the world can take the place of PERSISTENCE.
Talent will not.
Nothing is more common than unsuccessful people with talents.
Genius will not.
Unrewarded genius is almost a proverb.
Education will not.
The world is full of educated derelicts.
The slogan "Press On!" has solved and always will solve
The problems of the human race.

Turning people on

We have heard people saying, "Talk is cheap."

When we just talk about never giving up without taking any other action, then that's not good enough.

We all feel a little down on life occasionally. We need some encouragement once in a while.

What should we do?

We can help each other grow, in wisdom, in love.

As we discussed earlier, love is the will to extend one's self for the purpose of nurturing one's own or another's spiritual growth.

In his book, ***The 5 Love Languages,*** Gary Chapman reveals the secret to love that lasts. Gary Chapman, a great marriage counselor, asks:

How do we meet each other's deep emotional need to feel loved?

If we can learn that and choose to do that, then the love we share will be beyond anything we ever felt when we were infatuated.

The truth that may be missing is that we speak in different emotional love languages. Your emotional love language and the language of your spouse may be as different as Chinese from English.

For example, a man may love his wife by being sincere or by bringing home the bacon. But his wife view love slightly differently. Perhaps she is looking in his behavior and doesn't see it. Or perhaps she wants him to spend quality time with her. We must be willing to learn our spouse's primary love language.

There are five love languages:

- Words of affirmation
- Quality time
- Receiving gifts
- Acts of service
- Physical touch.

These five love languages can be adapted to be applied to a relationship between parent & child, siblings, friends, colleagues, and fellow activists.

We are the world

Be the change you want to see in the world. Let love go viral.

Harry Belafonte was moved to tears by all the violence and

poverty in Africa. He wanted to put together a benefit concert featuring black musicians to raise money for Africa. Ken Kragan was president of the organization United Support of Artists for Africa. Belafonte spoke to Kragan. But Kragan thought that an American version of "Band Aid" would be a better idea.

Ken Kragan owned a personal management and TV production company with Lionel Ritchie as one of his clients. Kragan phoned Ritchie to share his idea. Ritchie shared the idea with his wife who then talked to Steve Wonder's wife. She arranged to line Wonder up for the song.

As news spread, Quincy Jones was lined up as the producer. Michael Jackson and Lionel Ritchie agreed to write the song. They all agreed that in order to make sure that most of the artists would be free on a single date, the recording would take place on the night of the American Music Awards on January 28, 1985.

The instrumental tracks which were recorded ahead of time were sent to all the interested musicians. That night they performed with awesome power.

800,000 copies arrived in stores on Tuesday March 7, 1985. They were sold out by the first weekend. It shot up the charts. It won a Grammys in 1985 for Song of the Year and Record of the Year.

Here are the lyrics of that awesome song ***We Are The World, USA for Africa***:

There comes a time when we need a certain call
When the world must come together as one.
There are people dying
Oh, and it's time to lend a hand to life
The greatest gift of all.

We can't go on pretending day by day
That someone, somehow will soon make a change

We're a part of God's great big family
And the truth - you know love is all we need

(CHORUS)
We are the world, we are the children
We are the ones who make a brighter day
So let's start giving.
There's a choice we're making
We're saving our own lives
It's true we'll make a better day
Just you and me.

Well, send'em you your heart
So they know that someone cares
And their lives will be stronger and free
As God has shown us.
By turning stone to bread
And so we all must lend a helping hand.

(CHORUS)

When you you're down and out
There seems no hope at all.
But if you just believe
There's no way we can fall.
Well, well, well, let's realize
That one change can only come
When we stand together as one.

We are the world, we are the children
We are the ones who make a brighter day
So let's start giving.
There's a choice we're making
We're saving our own lives
It's true we'll make a better day
Just you and me.

Enjoying the journey

Even though we are enjoying the journey, in an odyssey of lifelong learning from our mistakes, be prepared for ***a long and bumpy ride.*** Therefore, be prepared to tough it out to the very end.

Never ever give up part way. If you are already halfway there, don't ever turn around and go back. Don't rely on your talents, genius, education, or money. Let your spirit lead you. Remember money can buy a house but not a home.

PRESS ON with hope in your heart and you'll never walk alone, for we are with you all the way:

Former president Calvin Coolidge says it best:

Nothing can take the place of ***PERSISTENCE.***
Talent will not.
Nothing is as common as unsuccessful people with talent.
Genius will not.
Unrewarded genius is almost a proverb.
Education will not.
The world is full of educated derelicts.
*The slogan "****PRESS ON!****" has solved and always will solve*
The problems of the human race.

To help you keep going when the going gets tough, always remember that ***you'll never walk alone.*** Hum this song, and soon others who are sharing the same pain and struggles of life as you, will join you in spirit, in song, and in taking action to pursue the same vision of a better world.

You'll Never Walk Alone is a show tune from the 1945 Rodgers & Hammerstein musical ***Carousel***. In the second act of the musical, Nettie Fowler, the cousin of the protagonist Julie Jordan, sings ***"You'll Never Walk Alone"*** to comfort and encourage

Julie when her husband, Billy Bigelow, the male lead, falls on his knife and dies after a failed robbery attempt.

In the final scene of ***Carousel***, in the commencement ceremony, Louise (Billy and Julie's daughter) remain quiet and sad even when the audience was singing the song. The now invisible Billy was granted a chance to return to earth for this one special day in order to redeem himself and silently motivate his daughter, the unhappy Louise, to join in the song.

This song inspire so much emotions that it is sung almost everywhere - in concerts, Emmy Awards nights, anniversaries and of course in association football clubs like Liverpool, Dortmund, Celtics, FC Twente, Feyenoord, SC Canbuur, Club Brugge and so forth.

*Here's the lyrics of **You'll Never Walk Alone:***

When you walk through a storm
Hold your head up high
And don't be afraid of the dark.
At the end of a storm
There's a golden sky
And the sweet silver song of a lark.
Walk on through the wind
Walk on through the rain
Though your dreams be tossed and blown.
Walk on, walk on
With hope in your heart
And you'll never walk alone.
You'll never walk alone.
Walk on, walk on
With hope in your heart
And you'll never walk alone
You'll never walk alone.

Your loved ones who have gone to heaven are whispering in your heart encouraging you to PRESS ON to fight until the war is won.

The best rendition, in my view, is by Gerry and the Pacemakers YouTube video:

Gerry & the Pacemaker - You'll Never Walk Alone (Official video)

Some of you may be saying that the range of this song is too wide. Don't worry. In his book, ***Your Erroneous Zones,*** Dr. Wayne W Dyer talks about people's erroneous zones - infuriating little quirks of personality that are barriers to a fuller, richer life.

Similarly, when it comes to singing your favorite songs, (like ***We are the World***, and ***You'll never walk alone***), you may also find barriers in your throat and tongue that stop you from achieving a fuller, richer singing voice. Do you want free singing lessons online?

Then go watch this ***YouTube video by Madeleine Harvey*** to get a taste of how beautiful your natural voice really is in a very short time:

How to free your singing voice when you sing

Then compare that approach to Ken Tamplin's approach by working on singing just five vowels first to keep your inner space open (Spoken English has more than 12 vowels):

How To Sing Any Song - Voice Lessons - Ken Tamplin Vocal Academy

Act now on your beliefs

A disunited people is too weak to do anything meaningful. But the people, united, cannot be defeated. Here are several ways your A-Team can bond together:

- **Share the same vision of a better world**, where nations and individuals embrace the agreement of peaceful co-existence and non-alignment. Don't micromanage. State your objective and allow others to achieve it in their own unique and creative ways. Be generous with your praise and stingy with your criticism.

- **Use the same mental models** - *The 7 Habits of Highly Effective People, The 6 Rules that Jack Welch live by, The Road Less Traveled, Maximum Success* and so forth.
- **Use the Six Thinking Hats** when you discuss and make decisions (don't waste your time arguing; kick your ego from the throne of your heart; let principle sit on the throne; be centered in principles, values, and virtues),
- **Sing your group's theme songs** - such as ***We Are The World*** and ***You'll Never Walk Alone.***

For you to make ***the living democracy movement*** a fighting force and make your nation and family great again, you must stay united. You must stand together as ONE.

Listen more, argue less. Seek first to understand others. Develop empathy and synergy. Practice creative cooperation. Always use the ***Six Thinking Hats*** to discuss before making important decisions. Be a great team player. Unity is strength. Be united and stay united. Dine, play and sing together. Share the same vision with your fellow activists in ***the living democracy movement.***

Aristotle is right and wise when he said this:

We are what we repeatedly do. Excellence then, is not an act, but a HABIT.

The enemy of your enemy can be your friend.

Evil flourish when good people who know do nothing.

Decisions have the power to steer and change your life forever.

Therefore, nothing affects the quality of your life than your ability to make the right decisions. All that you have achieved or failed to achieved can be traced back to the decisions you've made - on issues concerning your vote, health, wealth, relationships, and life purpose.

Change your beliefs, and you will change your principles, values, virtues, habits, attitudes, social skills, ethics, behavior and so forth.

In life there are no mistakes, only lessons. The secret to resilience, happiness and a less stressful success is to avoid focusing on stagnant traits. Instead, focus on adopting an active, growth-oriented and problem-solving approach to life, and enjoying the journey together with your loved ones.

Here are the beliefs of greatness that will empower you to enjoy the journey with your loved ones:

- That which is hateful to you, do not do to your fellow human beings. Any interpretation of scriptures that bred hatred or disdain for others - whatever their beliefs - is illegitimate. (Hillel)
- True religion is protecting the powerless - orphans, widows, homeless, migrant workers, disabled, and injured soldiers returning from an unnecessary war.
- Power without love is reckless and abusive. Love without power is sentimental and anemic. Power at its best is love implementing the demands of justice. Justice at its best is power correcting everything that stands against love. (Martin Luther King)
- That which matter most must never be at the mercy of things that matter least. (Goethe)
- Courage is not the absence of fear but rather the judgment that something is more important than fear. The brave may

not live forever. But the cautious do not live at all. (Meg Cabot)

- So long as you open your heart to beauty, hope, cheer, courage and power, so long are you young. (Samuel Ulman). I know of no more encouraging fact than the unquestionable ability of man to elevate his life by conscious endeavor (Henry David Thoreau).
- We should encourage each other to follow the rules of considerate conduct such as think before we act, listen more, argue less, seek first to understand, think twice before asking favors, avoid shifting responsibility and blame, avoid jumping to conclusions, respect other's opinion, and enjoying the journey with your loved ones.
- If you want to achieve what you've never achieved before, you have to grow to become what you've never become before. (Brian Tracy). Insanity is doing the same over and over again and expecting different results. No problem can be solved at the same level of consciousness that created it. (Albert Einstein)
- Success and cheerfulness in life are not the result of what we have but rather how we live. What we do with the things we already have now makes the biggest difference in the quality of our life. (Tony Robbins)
- Studies have shown that companies hire for attitude and train for skills. (Singapore Airlines).
- Humility is the beginning of wisdom. (Zen habits)
- A foolish definition of success is the attainment of a certain amount of money, power, and privilege. A wise definition of success is enjoying the journey of lifelong learning with your loved ones.
- All men are created equal, endowed with the unalienable

rights to life, liberty and the pursuit of happiness. (US Declaration of Independence)

- The world will be safer and prosperous when all nations adhere to the principles of peaceful coexistence where there is mutual respect for each other's territorial sovereignty and the right to self-determination and non-interference. (China-India)
- Whether a cat is black or white makes no difference. A cat that catches mice is a good cat. Whether we label an ideology socialism, capitalism, communism, or authoritarianism makes no difference. A government that can provide affordable subsidized public housing, meaningful jobs, efficient transport system, clean environment, fantastic schools, universal health care, recreation centers, and national security is a good government and should be given a strong mandate to govern. (Deng Xiaoping)
- Every nation must strive to avoid contracting the national disease of schizophrenia where there are two equally dominant sectarian political parties, bickering with each other like two juveniles. It is best if there is a political party that promote universal values that protect the rights of minorities so as to gain at least 70% of popular vote thus attaining a strong mandate to govern.
- Workers must enjoy democracy at the workplace where they have a say in the management of the company and reserve the right to buy the company if the owners decide to sell.
- All citizens must have a fair share in the prosperity of the nation. This can be achieved by practicing universal basic income (UBI) calculated as a small percentage of the living wage. UBI is able to soften the ills of neoliberalism by reducing the pain and frustration of the underprivileged who are the victims of the wealth gap between the rich and the poor. UBI is able to reduce the risk of violent civil unrest.

- Every citizen must be given universal healthcare.
- Every person has the right to demand privacy, especially when he or she has not committed any crime. (Edward Snowden)
- Every person has the right to choose his own way of life without being judged or criticized so long as he or she respects the rule of law. He can choose voluntary simplicity, country living, living off the grid, any profession, urban competition, climbing the corporate ladder, activism, the military, or politics.
- Whistleblowers should be protected by law when they expose the wrongdoings within the company or government.

Chapter four

CORRUPTION

Corruption may be defined as a dishonest or unethical conduct by a person entrusted with a position of authority that leads to personal benefit which conflict with his responsibility in that position of authority.

This means that where there is a conflict of interest, that person, to stay honest and ethical must choose either to keep his position and reject the benefit or resign and deal with the benefit.

Corruption may include many activities such as fake news, monopoly, tax evasion, vote-buying, kickbacks, bribery, embezzlement, theft, fraud, extortion, blackmail, networking, abuse of power, favoritism, nepotism, clientism, fraudulent endorsement of products or point of view, organized crime, and religious fraud.

In her book, ***Thieves of State***, Sarah Chayes explains why corruption threatens global security. Money speaks louder than virtue. The common thread that runs through geopolitical events is corruption.

Corruption featured highly in many global events such as the invasion of Iraq, the hostility towards Iran, the invasion of Syria, the support for Israel, the abduction of school girls in Nigeria, and the Afghanistan war.

Corruption also featured highly in why the US military budget is many times bigger than most countries - because war is big business, presenting plenty of opportunities for kickbacks.

Corruption is also highly featured in why the US back away from the Paris Agrement on Climate Change so as to appease workers in the fossil fuel sector.

Corruption is also highly featured in why medical expenses in the US are ten times higher than the medical expenses in Canada.

Corruption also featured highly in why the Republicans and Democrats are bickering with each other over bills that could have made the US great again. Every official is protecting his or her own sectarian tuft.

Neoliberalism

Corruption is also widespread in academia. Academics are paid to support neoliberalism. They brainwashed the masses with their theories to make them believe that the best government is a small government, that governments should not interfere with free enterprise and the activities of corporations - that is, if you want to see the economy continue to grow (which is a myth).

Neoliberalism is an evil dogma that is offered as a powerful way to boost the economy by transferring economic power from the government to the private sector and let the market rule the economy.

Neoliberalism helps rig the financial system, allowing corporations to rule the world. Neoliberalism construct a moral code that feeds fraud and corruption. Volkswagen for example can get away with falsifying emission certification for some time before it was discovered because of corruption.

Scientific American was alleged to have been bribed to come out in support of the safety of GMO foods. Similar fraud has been discovered in many sectors including the banking system, arms industry, and health care.

Corporate fraud does not exist just in developed countries. It is present in almost all countries, to various degrees. Corruption is so entrenched that even public censure does not pose a threat to banks, the military or any other sector.

Trying to make sense of all these economic practices will give the masses headache. Unless your have an equally strong case to go against the super-brain arrogance, you might as well stay silent. So the masses simply complain a little, feel powerless, and continue to struggle through the day.

Panama papers

In 2012, James Henry, former chief economist at the consultancy McKinsey published a new report. This McKinsey report revealed that around the world, the extremely wealthy had accumulated at least $21 trillion in secretive offshore accounts. This was a sum that was equal to the GDP of the US and Japan added together.

In 2015, 11.5 million documents were leaked by an anonymous source, now known as John Doe. These leaked documents detailed financial and attorney-client information for more than 214,488 offshore entities. These were known as the ***Panama Papers*** because they came from the Panamanian law firm and corporate service provider Mossack Fonseca.

These documents contained personal financial information about wealthy individuals and public officials that were kept private and confidential. While offshore business entities are legal, they become illegal if these shell companies are used for illegal purposes such as fraud, tax evasion, and evading international sanctions.

John Doe, the whistleblower, leaked these documents to German journalist Bastian Obermayer, deputy head on the investigative unit of the newspaper Siddeutsche Zeitung (SZ) based in Munich.

Russian oligarch

Obermayer had been awarded the ACFE Guardian Award during an international conference in Austin. The inscription on the trophy read: *For Vigilance in Fraud Reporting.* But Obermayer was not present at the conference to receive this award because he was involved in another major ongoing case involving a Russia oligarch.

Obermayer said:

I'm very sad that I can't be with you. I feel very honored to receive the Guardian Award. I am especially proud of the award's inscription, ***For Vigilance in Fraud Reporting****. That's exactly what we liked to do in the last number of years. We tried to have a very close look at the powerful and see what we can find out about fraud and corruption.*

Investigating fraud and corruption is hard and difficult. Very often it's annoying and it's expensive. And it's a problem especially for journalism. And that's why I'm proud we can still do this.

This work has been gratifying because we had seen real political and legislative change in so many nations because of their journalistic efforts.

We have to show the people that their rage and anger about corruption and fraud is not unseen. We have to hold the powerful accountable.

An anonymous source had delivered a 7-hour 2017 video to Obermayer. It revealed that Austrian Vice Chancellor, who had since resigned, offered public contracts to a woman, purported to be a niece of a Russian oligarch, in exchange for political backing for his reelection. The coalition Austrian government collapsed in May 2017.

Thanks to investigative journalists like Obermayer, mass protests happened everywhere - in Austria, Argentina, France, the UK and Iceland.

Obermayer has received numerous awards and has authored several books including ***The Panama Papers:*** *Breaking the Story of How the Rich and Powerful Hide Their Money.*

Lobbying

Lobbying is an act of attempting to influence decisions made by officials in a government, most often legislators or members of regulatory agencies.

Lobbying is done by many types of individuals from associations, organized groups, business executives, and colleagues. There are also individuals who do lobbying as a profession.

Lobbying is a double-edged sword. It can be used for or against corruption. Lobbying has the potential for conflicts of interest. It is prevalent in all countries. In many countries, lobbying can be a profession made respectable by the presence of many lawyers and accountants. In many countries, a lobbyist can gain entry into legislature buildings by application signed by two lawmakers or councillors.

Jack Allan Abramoff, born February 28, 1959, is an American lobbyist, businessman, movie producer, and writer. Abramoff was College Republican National Committee National Chairman from 1981 to 1985. He was a founding member of the

International Freedom Foundation. He served on the board of directors of the National Center for Public Policy Research, a conservative think tank.

From 1994 to 2001, Abramoff was the top lobbyist for the firm of Preston Gates & Ellis, and then for Greenberg Traurig until March 2004 when he was under investigation together with 21 other individuals. Those investigated testified before the Senate Indian Affairs Committee in September, 2004. He pleaded guilty.

Abramoff was also investigated in his dealings with SunCruz Casinos in January 2006. He was found guilty of mail fraud, conspiracy to bribe public officials, and tax evasion. Abramoff was sentenced to six years in jail. He served 43 months and was released on December 3, 2010.

While in prison, he wrote his biography about his life as a crooked lobbyist in ***Capitol Punishment:*** *the hard truth about Washington corruption from America's most notorious lobbyist.*

Abramoff went on to make two films in 2010: a documentary *Casino Jack and the United States of Money*, released in May 2010, and the feature film *Casino Jack*, released on December 17, 2010, starring Kevin Spacey as Abramoff.

Abramoff was a master at showering gifts on lawmakers in return for their votes on legislation and tax breaks favorable to his clients. Abramoff was so good at lobbying that he took home $20 million a year.

Abramoff was so far into these corrupt practices that he couldn't figure out where right and wrong was. He believed that he was among the top moral people in the business of lobbying. He was oblivious and blinded by what was really going on.

Abramoff was thinking of writing a book - The Idiot's Guide to Buying a Congressman. Most congressmen don't think they were being bought. They felt that the system allowed them to receive gifts from others. There was no disincentives in the system to guide behavior.

Abramoff would lavish certain congressmen and senators with access to private jets and junkets to the world's great golf destinations like St. Andrews in Scotland. Abramoff gave free meals at his own upscale Washington restaurant and access to the best tickets to all the area's sporting events, including two skyboxes at Washington Redskins games.

Abramoff spent more than $1 million a year on tickets to sporting events and concerts He had two people on his staff doing full-time booking tickets.

State-owned enterprises (SOEs)

Controlled by national governments, SOEs rank among the largest companies in the world. They also serve as some of the biggest employers in their country.

SOEs are central to the daily lives of citizens, providing critical goods and services in many sectors such as transport, utilities, telecommunications, and health. Here is where the public sector can counter the ills of capitalism where corporations rule the world - provided the government officials themselves are not corrupt or incompetent.

SOEs have specific corruption risks because of its close ties with governments and public officials. For example, the state oil company in Brazil Petrobras was found guilty of a major corruption scandal. The Nordic telecoms giant Telia was recently caught bribing for business in Uzbekistan and was fined $965 million.

Still, if governments want to really serve the people, using SOEs, as representatives of the people, to compete with listed companies will be a powerful way to stabilize prices, sustain the environment, and fund the social programs that protect the interests of the working class.

Transparency International works with governments, businesses, and citizens to stop the abuse of power, bribery, and secret deals. From villages in India to the corridors of power in major cities, Transparency International gives voice to the victims and witnesses of corruption. Transparency International is a global movement that wants a world free of corruption.

An unprecedented anti-corruption campaign was launched immediately after the conclusion of the 18th National Congress of the Communist Party of China held in Beijing in November, 2012.

President Xi Jinping vowed to crackdown on "tigers and flies," that is, high officials and local civil servants alike. Those who were found guilty of bribery, abuse of power and other wrongdoings.

Wang Qishan, head of the 18th Central Commission for Discipline Inspection is in charge of this anti-corruption campaign. It netted over 120 high-ranking officials, military officers, several senior executives of SOEs, and five national leaders. More than 100,000 people were indicted for corruption.

More than 1,000 Chinese fugitives who fled abroad were returned to China in 2019 and more than $519 million in ill-gotten gains was recovered.

Anti-corruption agencies

An anti-corruption agency is a special police agency specialized in fighting political corruption and engaging in general anti-corruption activities. Most are founding by statute, but some have a constitutional status.

The United Nations Convention Against Corruption (UNCAC) is

the only legally binding international anti-corruption multilateral treaty. Negotiated by member states of the United Nations, it has been adopted by the UN General Assembly in October 2003, and entered into force in 2005

The anti-corruption sites in the United States are as follows:

Department of Commerce - Office of General Counsel

Department of Commerce - Trade Compliance Center

Department of State - Bureau of International Narcotics and Law Enforcement Affairs

Department of State - Bureau of Energy, Economic and Business Affairs

Securities and Exchange Commission

The anti-corruption sites in China are as follows:

National Supervisory Commission (Central Commission for Discipline Inspection)

Commission for Discipline Inspection of the Central Military Commission

Independent Commission Against Corruption (HOng Kong)

Commission Against Corruption (Macau)

Transparency International is an international non-governmental organization (NGO) which is based in Berlin, Germany. It was founded in 1993. Its nonprofit purpose is to take action to combat global corruption. It proposes civil societal anti-corruption measures and ways to prevent criminal activities arising from corruption

Corruption impacts the poorest and most vulnerable in society the hardest.

Ordinary citizens suffer the most when the corrupt steal funds that was intended for public services like infrastructure, healthcare, and education.

One in four people around the world say they had to pay a bribe to access public services in the past twelve months. But ordinary people can fight back against corruption. Ordinary people can make a real difference.

For example, in Clinique de las Flores, Guatemala, dirty water flowing out of the taps made many children sick. Residents were forced to buy clean water. They turned to the municipality for help but was met with a brickwall. They turned to Accion Ciudadana of Transparency International.

Transparency International investigated this matter. It uncovered a trail of corruption that led to ghost workers and a dead man being paid to construct water pipes.

Sindy Celeste Rodas Carbonell organized a petition and march for new elections. The corrupt mayor was removed from office and residents got their clean water.

The untouchables

During the 19th century in the US, alcoholism, family violence, and saloon-based corruption were rampant. Protestants were up in arms to stop this deterioration in society. This prompted the ban on the production, import, transport and sale of alcoholic beverages from 1920 to 1933. This ban was known as the Prohibition.

The Prohibition, enforced under the Volstead Act, set down the rules for enforcing the federal ban and defined the types of alcohol beverages that were prohibited.

Criminal gangs were able to gain control of the beer and liquor supply under the prohibition.

The Untouchables is a 1987 American gangster movie that follows the life of Eliot Ness as he forms ***The Untouchables*** team to bring down Al Capone to justice during the Prohibition.

During the Prohibition, Al Capone was the crime kingpin supplying illegal liquor in the entire city of Chicago. The US Department of Justice tasked Eliot Ness with bringing a stop to Capone's activities. Ness's first attempt at a liquor raid on Capone failed due to corrupt cops tipping Capone off.

Eliot Ness had a chance meeting with a veteran Irish-American cop named Jim Malone. Malone was fed up with the rampant corruption in Chicago. He offered to help Ness. Malone suggested that Ness find a man from the police academy who had not been corrupted by Capone.

Malone and Ness spotted Italian-American trainee Guiseppe Petri aka George Stone. They handpicked Petri because of his superior marksmanship and integrity. Washington DC assigned Oscar Wallace as their accountant.

The Untouchables team conducted a successful raid on a Capone liquor cache. They receive enthusiastic public coverage and support. Capone killed the person in charge of the cache as a warning to his other subordinates.

Wallace the accountant for ***The Untouchables*** team discovered that Capone had not filed an income tax return for the last four years. Wallace suggested that the team should build up a tax evasion case against Capone to put him away for good.

Capone sent a man to meet Ness and offered a bribe if he could drop his investigation. Ness rejected the bribe. Capone then sent his enforcer Frank Nitti to threaten Ness's family. Ness immediately moved his wife and daughter to a safe house.

The Untouchables team made another raid on the Canadian border. They killed several gangsters and captured Capone's bookkeeper named George. Ness eventually managed to persuade George to collaborate and testify against Capone.

Wallace escorted George from the Police Station to a safe house. But on the way, both were killed by Nitti, Capone's enforcer. Ness rushed to the Lexington Hotel to confront Capone, but Malone intervened because they were outnumbered. Malone urged Ness to focus on working on the tax evasion case.

Malone found out that police chief Mike Dorsett sold out Wallace and George. Malone fought with Dorsett, won, and forced him to reveal the whereabouts of Capone's head bookkeeper, Walter Payne.

That evening, when Malone was home, he was lured out of is apartment by Nitti's underling. Malone was then fatally wounded by Nitti at close range. When Ness visited Malone, he found him on the floor covered with blood. Before he died, Malone informed Ness that Capone's head bookkeeper Payne was about to take a train out of town from Union Station.

Ness and Stone rushed to Union Station. The eventual shootout at Union Station was made more complicated by the presence of two bystanders, a woman and her child in a pram. Still, Ness and Stone managed to capture Payne and killed his escorts.

At the Capone trial, Ness observed that Capone was strangely calm. Then he noticed that Nitti, who was there, was wearing a gun. Ness indicated to the bailiff to remove Nitti from the court room. The bailiff searched Nitti and found the gun he was wearing. But Nitti said he had a permit issued by Chicago's mayor, William Hale Thompson.

Ness was present when the bailiff searched Nitti. Ness found a matchbook. When he flipped up the flap, Ness saw Malone's apartment number written on it. Ness then knew that Nitti was Malone's killer. He chased after Nitti, and eventually forced him off the roof of the building. Nitti crashed onto a car below.

On the street, Stone retrieved a list from Nitti's coat. This list showed all the names of the jurors. Ness knew that the jurors in the Capone trial had been bribed.

In the courtroom, during recess, Ness met with the judge, and indirectly hinted that his name was on a Capone list. The judge was forced to follow Ness's suggestion to switch the jury with the jury from another court. This prompted Capone's lawyer to plead guilty. Capone rushed forward to punch his lawyer but was held back by his aides.

Capone was found guilty of tax evasion and sentenced to eleven years in jail. On the day Capone began serving his sentence, Ness closed up his office. He handed Malone's St. Jude medallion and callbox key to Stone as a farewell gift.

Multiple choice

HOW IMPORTANT ARE THE DECISIONS YOU MAKE?

Decisions have the power to steer and change your life forever. Therefore, nothing affects the quality of your life more than your ability to make the right decisions. All that you have achieved or failed to achieved can be traced back to the decisions you've made - on issues concerning your vote, health, wealth, relationships, and life purpose.

In his book, ***BLINK, the power of thinking without thinking***, Malcolm Gladwell proves that great decision-makers aren't those who process the most information or spend the most time deliberating, but those who have perfected the art of "thin-slicing" - knowing the very few things that matter.

This HANDBOOK will reveal to you the few things that matter

most, such as answering these most important questions:

- How can I enjoy the journey in such a messy world?
- How would the US-China 21st century war impact my life?
- How can I take my life back from corporate dominance?
- How do good people make tough decisions?
- What is a wise definition of success?

When General Electric faced fierce competition from Japanese and South Korean corporations in the 1980s, it was a matter of fight or sink. He was chosen from 12 shortlisted senior executives to succeed Reg Jones. He was a man on a life-and-death mission, He led General Electric as if GE was on the brink of bankruptcy.

Jack Welch lived by these six rules:

- Control your destiny or someone else will.
- Face reality as it is, not as it was, or a you wish it were.
- Be candid with everyone.
- Don't manage. Lead.
- Change before you have to.
- If you don't have competitive advantage, don't compete.

I'm sure these six rules will help you make great decisions.

There are at least two main options for you to choose from when you face a situation or crisis: fight or run, stay or leave, give up or press on, negotiate or stay firm, change or stay stubborn.

Usually, if you think hard enough, you can generate more options which combine the best elements of both roads. If you can do that, why not give it a try. If one door closed on you, another door will pop open.

That's why Robert Frost's poem resonates with almost everyone. However, be careful how you interpret this poem. It doesn't mean that one road is better than the other. It only means that as human beings, you cannot take every road you meet. It isn't a matter of right or wrong. It has more to do with thinking before you act. Act when you feel it is more advantageous for you - either in the short term, long term or both. You cannot stagnate at the junction all your life. You have got to JUST DO IT AND CORRECT COURSE ALONG THE WAY.

So here's Robert Frost's provocative poem:

Two roads diverged in a yellow wood,
And sorry I could not travel both
And be one traveler, long I stood.
And looked down one as far as I could
To where it bent in the undergrowth.

Then took the other, as just as fair,
And having perhaps the better claim,
Because it was grassy and wanted wear.
Though as for that passing there
Had worn them really about the same.

And both that morning equally lay
In leaves, no step had trodden black.
Oh, I kept the first for another day!
Yet knowing how way leads on to way,
I doubted if I should ever come back.

I shall be telling this with a sigh
Somewhere ages and ages hence:
Two roads diverged in a wood, and I -
I took the one less traveled by,
And that has made all the difference.

Even though we are enjoying the journey, in an odyssey of lifelong learning from our mistakes, be prepared for a long long journey. Therefore, be prepared to tough it out to the very end. Never ever give up part way. If you are already halfway there, don't ever turn around and go back. Press on with hope in your heart and you'll never walk alone, for we are with you all the way:

Former president Calvin Coolidge says it best:

Nothing can take the place of ***PERSISTENCE.***
Talent will not.
Nothing is as common as unsuccessful people with talent.
Genius will not.
Unrewarded genius is almost a proverb.
Education will not.
The world is full of educated derelicts.
*The slogan "**PRESS ON!**" has solved and always will solve*
The problems of the human race.

Act now on your beliefs

In his book, ***The Corporation: the pathological pursuit of profit and power,*** Joel Bakan reveals that over the past 150 years, the corporation has risen from relative obscurity to become the world's dominant economic institution.

Today's corporation is a pathological institution, a dangerous possessor of the great power it wields over people and societies. It's self-interest victimizes individuals, society, and the environment.

However, it is not the corporation's fault. The fault lies in the government and civil society not doing their part sufficiently well to harness its power to do good.

Government fears civil unrest. Corporations fear customer revolt. We, the people, when united, can impose incentives and disincentives to guide the behavior of corporations so that they will not rule the world without or consent and benefit.

Get involved in the anti-corruption narrative in your country. Be the change you want to see in the world. Stand united, for unity is strength. Government fear civil unrest. Corporations fear customer revolt. You the people, when united, can spring clean your nation and make it great again.

Get inspired by watching the documentary YouTube video: ***The Corporation***.

Flood corrupt corporations, government departments, and agencies with letters, email and social media comments to show your stand:
(Example)

Dear Sir/Madam:

I have been buying your wonderful products. But since I have discovered your non-compliance, I have decided to stop buying your products and persuade my family, neighbors, colleagues, and friends to do the same unless you show us you care about your customers and rectify this error...

Decisions have the power to steer and change your life forever. Therefore, nothing affects the quality of your life than your ability to make the right decisions. All that you have achieved or failed to achieved can be traced back to the decisions you've made - on issues concerning your vote, health, wealth, relationships, and life purpose.

Change your beliefs, and you will change your principles, values, virtues, habits, attitudes, social skills, ethics, behavior and so forth.

In life there are no mistakes, only lessons. The secret to resilience, happiness and a less stressful success is to avoid focusing on stagnant traits. Instead, focus on adopting an active, growth-oriented and problem-solving approach to life, and enjoying the journey together with your loved ones.

Here are the beliefs of greatness that will empower you to enjoy the journey with your loved ones:

- That which is hateful to you, do not do to your fellow human beings. Any interpretation of scriptures that bred hatred or disdain for others - whatever their beliefs - is illegitimate. (Hillel)
- True religion is protecting the powerless - orphans, widows, homeless, migrant workers, disabled, and injured soldiers returning from an unnecessary war.
- Power without love is reckless and abusive. Love without power is sentimental and anemic. Power at its best is love implementing the demands of justice. Justice at its best is power correcting everything that stands against love. (Martin Luther King)
- That which matter most must never be at the mercy of things that matter least. (Goethe)
- Courage is not the absence of fear but rather the judgment that something is more important than fear. The brave may not live forever. But the cautious do not live at all. (Meg Cabot)
- So long as you open your heart to beauty, hope, cheer, courage and power, so long are you young. (Samuel Ulman). I know of no more encouraging fact than the unquestionable ability of man to elevate his life by conscious endeavor (Henry David Thoreau).
- We should encourage each other to follow the rules of con-

siderate conduct such as think before we act, listen more, argue less, seek first to understand, think twice before asking favors, avoid shifting responsibility and blame, avoid jumping to conclusions, respect other's opinion, and enjoying the journey with your loved ones.

- If you want to achieve what you've never achieved before, you have to grow to become what you've never become before. (Brian Tracy). Insanity is doing the same over and over again and expecting different results. No problem can be solved at the same level of consciousness that created it. (Albert Einstein)
- Success and cheerfulness in life are not the result of what we have but rather how we live. What we do with the things we already have now makes the biggest difference in the quality of our life. (Tony Robbins)
- Studies have shown that companies hire for attitude and train for skills. (Singapore Airlines).
- Humility is the beginning of wisdom. (Zen habits)
- A foolish definition of success is the attainment of a certain amount of money, power, and privilege. A wise definition of success is enjoying the journey of lifelong learning with your loved ones.
- All men are created equal, endowed with the unalienable rights to life, liberty and the pursuit of happiness. (US Declaration of Independence)
- The world will be safer and prosperous when all nations adhere to the principles of peaceful coexistence where there is mutual respect for each other's territorial sovereignty and the right to self-determination and non-interference. (China-India)
- Whether a cat is black or white makes no differ-

ence. A cat that catches mice is a good cat. Whether we label an ideology socialism, capitalism, communism, or authoritarianism makes no difference. A government that can provide affordable subsidized public housing, meaningful jobs, efficient transport system, clean environment, fantastic schools, universal health care, recreation centers, and national security is a good government and should be given a strong mandate to govern. (Deng Xiaoping)

- Every nation must strive to avoid contracting the national disease of schizophrenia where there are two equally dominant sectarian political parties, bickering with each other like two juveniles. It is best if there is a political party that promote universal values that protect the rights of minorities so as to gain at least 70% of popular vote thus attaining a strong mandate to govern.
- Workers must enjoy democracy at the workplace where they have a say in the management of the company and reserve the right to buy the company if the owners decide to sell.
- All citizens must have a fair share in the prosperity of the nation. This can be achieved by practicing universal basic income (UBI) calculated as a small percentage of the living wage. UBI is able to soften the ills of neoliberalism by reducing the pain and frustration of the underprivileged who are the victims of the wealth gap between the rich and the poor. UBI is able to reduce the risk of violent civil unrest.
- Every citizen must be given universal healthcare.
- Every person has the right to demand privacy, especially when he or she has not committed any crime. (Edward Snowden)
- Every person has the right to choose his own way of life without being judged or criticized so long as he or she respects the rule of law. He can choose voluntary simplicity,

country living, living off the grid, any profession, urban competition, climbing the corporate ladder, activism, the military, or politics.

- Whistleblowers should be protected by law when they expose the wrongdoings within the company or government.

Chapter five

WARMONGERS

In 1577, Izaak Elchanan Rothschild was born in a house with a the red shield. At that time, houses were not numbered but were identified by its color or some symbol. This family and a few generations after that lived in the same house.

The Rothschild family ascent to international prominence began in 1744, with the birth of Mayer Amschel Rothschild in Frankfurt am Main, Germany.

Mayer was the son of Amschel Moses Rothschild, born around 1710, a money changer who traded with the Prince of Hesse. Mayer developed a finance house. Mayer was studying ways to insulate his family fortune from local mobs and greedy monarchs.

Mayer spread his empire by installing each of his five sons, Amschel, Salomon, Nathan, Calman, and Jacob, in the five main European financial centers to conduct business - Frankfurt, Vienna, London, Naples, and Paris. His strategy worked and his family fortune survived.

Napoleonic wars

At the start of the Napoleonic wars from 1803 to 1815, the

Rothschild family already possessed a significant fortune, gaining preeminence in the bullion trade at that time.

Nathan Mayer Rothschild almost single-handedly financed the British war effort. He organized shipment of bullion to assist the Duke of Wellington to wage war in Europe.

The five Rothschild brothers coordinated their logistics as well as their market trades, providing the best support to the British government ahead of their competitors.

The 18th century saw a mass migration from crowded Europe to the new world of North America. The thirteen British colonies declared their independence on July 4, 1776.

When the Rothschild family got insider information that the British would gain victory in Europe, they bought British government bonds and made a fairly huge fortune. Nathan Mayer Rothschild acquired the property at Number 2 New Court in St. Swithin's Lane as headquarters for his newly company, N M Rothschild & Sons in 1811.

In 1815, Nathan arranged a 5 million pound loan to the Prussian government. He also got approval to issue government bonds. By 1818, all the five brothers were elevated to the hereditary nobility by Austrian Emperor Francis I.

N M Rothschild & Sons had so much reserves that during the 1825-26 financial meltdown in the City of London, it was able to supply enough coin to the Bank of England to avert a market liquidity crisis. It practically pioneered international finance.

Bilderberg Meeting

The exploits of Napoleon led to the redrawing of the map of Europe. They provoked massive tensions. Minorities suffered ill treatment from dominant ethnic groups. Chief protagonists were Germany, France, and Prussia. Nations were scrambling around for raw materials from the Balkans, Asia, and Africa. This led to the two world wars.

The massive death toll from World War Two included 20 million Russians, 6 million Poles, 4 million Germans, 2 million Chinese, 2 million Japanese, and 1.7 million Yugoslavs. More than 21 million people were uprooted from their homes.

On August 21, 1944, diplomatic experts from the United States, United Kingdom, Soviet Union, and China met in Dumbarton Oaks, Washington DC. Their aim was to work out a proposed permanent organization to replace the League of Nations' mandate system to keep peace in the world

In June 1945, 50 nations signed the ***Charter of the United Nations***, which came into effect on October 24, 1945.

In 1954, 150 top leaders from North America and Europe were invited to a conference to augment the United Nations. Its objective was to have closed door frank discussions on global issues. Participants included political leaders, experts from many sectors such as industry, finance, academia, and the media.

The first meeting was held at Bilderberg Hotel in the Netherlands. It was chaired by Prince Bernhard of the Netherlands until 1976. The current chairman of the Bilderberg Meeting is Henri de Castries.

Attendees were entitled to use information gained at meetings but were not allowed to attribute it to a named speaker. This gave rise to many conspiracy theories about a new world order and one global government unelected by the people.

The 67th Bilderberg Meeting took place from May 30 to June 2, 2019 in Montreux, Switzerland. About 130 participants from 23 countries attended in their private capacity. The Chatham House Rule (UK think tank) was applied.

The key topics discussed in the 67th Bilder Meetingwere as follow:

- A stable strategic order
- What's next for Europe?
- Climate change and sustainability
- China
- Russia
- The future of capitalism
- Brexit
- The ethics of artificial intelligence
- The weaponisation of social media
- The importance of space
- Cyber threats

Corruption threatens global security

In her book, ***Thieves of State***, Sarah Chayes explains why corruption threatens global security.

According to Sarah Chayes, since the late 1990s, corruption has reached such an extent that some governments resemble glorified criminal gangs, bent solely on enriching themselves. These kleptocrats drive enraged populations to extremes - ranging from revolution to militant puritanical religion.

War is big business. Oil and precious metals are big business.

Corruption is the common cause that runs throughout the many disruptive events around the world:

- The wars in Iraq and Syria
- East-west standoff in Ukraine
- Abducted schoolgirls in Nigeria
- War in Afghanistan
- Arab spring
- Overthrow of the Mubarak government

Corruption can explain why the US and the CIA supported the Taliban, why they cooperated with the bin Laden family, why GH Bush was still in touch with them after he left office, why Dick Cheney moved from the private sector to become the US Vice President while retaining stocks in Halliburton, and so forth.

Daniel Ellsberg, born April 7, 1931, is an American economist, activist, and former US military analyst. He worked as a strategic analyst for Rand Corporation in 1957. His specialty was nuclear strategy and the command and control of nuclear weapons.

Ellberg left Rand to work in the Pentagon from August 1964 under Secretary of Defense Robert McNamara. Ellsberg then went to South Vietnam for two years. He returned to the US and resumed work at Rand. He was assigned to study classified documents on the conduct of the Vietnam War.

This study which Ellsberg worked on was known as the ***Pentagon Papers***. He was shocked at what he had discovered. Pentagon had been lying to the American people. The Vietnam War was not a fight against the communists. It was an unjust war where thousands of young men died in the battlefields.

Ellsberg attended several anti-war conferences. He was inspired by a draft resister named Randy Kehler who was prepared to go to prison rather than join an unjust war. Ellsberg rushed to an empty room and cried for an hour.

Ellsberg decided to release the ***Pentagon Papers*** to *The New York Times* and other newspapers in 1971. On January 3, 1973, the US government charged Ellsberg under the *Espionage Act of 1917* along with other charges of theft and conspiracy, that carried a maximum sentence of 115 years in prison.

Leonard Boudin and Harvard Law School Professor Charles Nesson came forward to defend Ellsberg. Due to governmental misconduct and illegal gathering of evidence, Judge William Matthew Byrne Jr dismissed all charges against Ellsberg on May 11, 1973.

Katharine Gun

On September 11, 2001, four passenger airliners operated by United Airlines and American Airlines departed from Northeastern US bound for California. 19 terrorists hijacked these four passenger airliners.

Two airliners crashed into the North and South 110-story towers of the World Trade Center in New York City. These two buildings collapsed in one hour and 42 minutes. They also brought down several of the surrounding buildings.

A third passenger crashed into the Pentagon, the headquarters of the US Department of Defense in Arlington County, Virginia, causing a partial collapse of the western wing of the Pentagon.

A fourth passenger airliner flew towards Washington DC, but crashed into an open field in Stonycreek Township near Shanksville, Pennsylvania.

These attacks, known as the 9/11 attacks, killed 2,996 people, injured 6,000 others. They caused at least $10 billion in property damage and $3 trillion in total costs. During the firefighting and rescue operations, 343 firefighters and 72 law enforcement officers died.

The US had urgent communications with UK and Australian governments. They believed that the terrorist group al-Qaeda must be behind these attacks. They were discussing ways to get the United Nations to sanction and attack on al-Qaeda and its leader Osama bin Laden.

At that time, 27-year-old Katharine Gun was working as a translator of Mandarin at the British government intelligence agency GCHQ in Cheltenham. In January, 2003, Katharine Gun was copied in a classified memo sent by a senior figure in the NSA to GCHQ.

The memo was a top-secret request to monitor the private communication of UN delegates for scraps of information, personal or otherwise, that could be used to "give the US an edge" in leveraging support for the invasion of Iraq.

Katharine was shocked. She decided to leak that memo to *The Observer*. Her intention was to try and help stop this invasion of Iraq. *The Observer* published the NSA top-secret memo on its front page in an issue just over two weeks before the Iraqi invasion.

To save her GCHQ colleagues from suffering a witch hunt, Katharine owned up to this leak. She was arrested and charged with breach of *The Official Secrets Act.*

Special branch officers asked Katharine why she had chosen to leak that memo, "You work for the British government."

"No. I work for the British people. I do not gather intelligence so the government can lie to the British people."

Katharine's whistleblowing did not avert the war. The US, UK, and also Australia colluded to fabricate excuses for the invasion of Iraq. In 2002, US President George Bush, UK Prime Minister Tony Blair, and Australian Prime Minister John Howard lied to their people, declaring the Saddam Hussein had stockpiles of chemical and biological weapons of mass destruction.

It seemed that the war in Iraq was not a mistake or a blunder. It was a war crime.

Ben Emmerson QC defended Katharine Gun. He asserted that the British government drop its charges against Katharine Gun. Otherwise, Emmerson would have to pursue the issue about whether it was lawful for the British government to participate in the invasion of Iraq. The British government relented and dropped the charges against Katharine Gun.

16 years later, Katharine Gun's most important words of courage still ring in the air:

"No. I work for the British people. I do not gather intelligence so the government can lie to the British people."

A movie, ***Official Secrets*** was made of her story. She was played by Keira Knightley.

Japan rearming

In 2019, Japan was close to passing a new law that allow it to engage in international conflict for the first time since World War Two. It was met with widespread protests against militarization in Japan.

The Japanese were proud of their country's pacifist tradition. Most of the public opposed the bill. They came out in droves to protest in front of the Japanese parliament in Tokyo.

If this bill is passed in Japan, then almost all countries are prepared to be involved in conflict.

The worst country in the world for external conflict was

Uganda Uganda was heavily involved in conflict in DR Congo as well as skirmishes with the Lord's Resistance Army (LRA) of Joseph Kony in border regions in Africa.

The US came second, followed by Rwanda, and then UK.

States that have the most nuclear weapons are Russia and the US, with 7,000 and 6,800 nuclear weapons respectively. Other nuclear states are France, China, UK, Pakistan, India, and Israel, each with less than 300 nuclear weapons.

It is not good logic for the US to say that if it pulls its troop out of Iraq and Iran, it will give rise to more terrorism. The reality is that the opposite is more true. The American sanctions on Iran is actually an act of war. This means that the US action is terrorist in nature, and most people in the Middle East look at US activities there as terrorist in nature.

This means that how Tulsi Gabbard explains about the Middle East situation is more sensible than the rhetoric of war hawks in the White House. When the majority of Muslims view American actions in the Middle East as hostile and unreasonable, it only give ISIS more justification to seek more support from fellow Muslims.

Middle east geopolitics

Islam is a monotheistic religion that descended from Abraham. Islam teaches that there is only one God (Allah) and that Prophet Muhammad is the Messenger of God (Allah).

There are 1.8 billion followers of Islam, most commonly known as Muslims, in the world. Muslims make up the majority of 50 countries, Muslims consider the Quran in its original Arabic to be the unaltered and final revelation of God. Prophet Muhammad followed the long line of prophets from Adam, Abraham, Moses, and Jesus.

Muslims make up 24% of the world population. 31% lives in South Asia, 20% in the Middle east and north Africa, 15% in Sub-Saharan Africa, 13% in Indonesia, and 21% in other parts of the world.

20% of 1.8 billion Muslims means that 360 million Muslims live in the Middle-east and north Africa. The League of Arab States, also known as the Arab League, formed on May 5, 1945, comprises 22 states. Its main aim is to draw closer the relations between member states and coordinate collaboration between them to safeguard their independence and sovereignty and to consider in a general way the affairs and interests of the Arab countries.

Prophet Muhammad (570 - 632) was called by Allah to destroy the 300 idols in Mecca and restore the worship of one true Allah.

All Muslims follow the five tenets if Islam:

- Muslims fast during Ramadan
- Muslims pledge to make a pilgrimage to Mecca at least once in his or her lifetime
- Muslims pray at least five times a day
- Muslims give charity to the poor
- Muslims pledge themselves to the Faith.

When Prophet Muhammad died in 632, his followers quarreled as to who should be his political successor. Most Muslims are of one of two denomination - Sunni (85%) or Shia (15%).

The Shiites are followers who believe that Muhammad's successor should come from his bloodline. The Sunnis are followers who believe that his successor can come from outside his bloodline.

Sunnis are dominant in Saudi Arabia, North Africa, and Indonesia. Shiites are dominant in Iran, Iraq, Syria, Lebanon, and Yemen.

The Middle East has huge reserves of oil. Big countries like the United States, Russia and China would like to have a piece of the action. However, their approaches are very different.

The United States has the most advanced technology to extract oil. Its oil companies were among the first to invest in the Middle East. Russia has similar intentions as the US but is less dominant. China takes the approach of having bilateral infrastructure projects under the Belt and Road Initiative.

Peoples in the region have little problem with their religious preferences. It was the giant corporations that politicize religion to have rival groups fight each other. War is good business for weapons manufacturers.

The four biggest countries in the Middle East are Saudi Arabia, Iran, Egypt, and Turkey in terms of land area.

Saudi Arabia has a land area of 2.2 million sq.km. It has a population of 34 million. Its GDP (N) is $779 billion. Saudi Arabia has an arrangement with the United States whereby all oil purchased from Saudi Arabia by any other country must be paid in US$. In turn, the US would give military protection to Saudi Arabia.

Iran, also called Persia, has a land area of 1.7 million sq.km. It has a population of 83 million. Its GDP (N) is $459 billion. Its relations with the US depends on whether its leader is moderate or radical.

Egypt has a land area of 1.0 million sq.km. It has a population of 100 million. Its GDP (N) is $302 billion.

Turkey has a land area of 783,356 sq.km. It has a population of 82 million. Its GDP (N) is $744 billion.

Iran has the best trained military among the four countries, known as the Islamic Revolutionary Guard. Iran vies with Saudi Arabia for supremacy in the Arab League.

US-Iran tensions

For those who don't know much about US and Iran history, it may help to watch this 5-minute YouTube video by Global News:

- ***US and Iran's rocky history explained in 5 minutes***

The Iran Nuclear Deal (Joint Comprehensive Plan of Action JCPOA) was signed by Iran and the US under President Obama in 2015 whereby the US would lift trade sanctions in exchange for Iran halting its nuclear program.

The reasoning behind this nuclear deal was that when Iran agrees to stop advancing its nuclear program, other countries like Saudi Arabia and United Arab Emirates would not start their own nuclear program.

But when President Trump took office, he broke off this Obama deal and put sanctions back on Iran. This put a terrible strain on Iran's economy. Inflation shot up 50%, and food prices shot up 85% in Iran.

According to the Pentagon, the US currently has 60,000 troops in the Middle East and North Africa. Tensions between Iran and the United States escalated dramatically after top Iranian commander Qassem Soleimani was assassinated in Iraq, ordered by US President Trump.

Iran retaliated with missile attacks on two Iraqi bases where US troops were stationed. Trump stated on TV that the US would fully strike back if Iran made further attacks on US citizens. The US had identified 52 sites it could hit back.

The US House of representatives and the Senate were not consulted on this. House Democrats planned a vote on a War Powers Resolution to limit the president's military actions regarding Iran.

The White House defended the the killing of Soleimani because he was planning an imminent attack on US forces in Iraq. Under the US Constitution, the authority to take military action is held by both Congress and the president. Congress has the power to declare war while the president, as commander-in-chief, has the power to use military to defend the US.

According to experts in constitutional law, the president does not have the authority to send troops to hostilities abroad without the explicit authorization of Congress..

World leaders and the United Nations urged the US and Iran to deescalate tensions. Meanwhile, millions of Iranians took to the streets to mourn the death of a very popular Iranian leader Qassem Soleimani. Protesters burned many US flags, vowing revenge over Soleimani assassination.

Iraqi parliament called on US and other foreign forces to leave. The US commander in Iraq said US troops would be preparing to leave. However, there were conflicting reports from the White House stating that US troops are not leaving Iraq. In the meantime, Iraq and Iran are moving closer together, willing to put aside their differences to battle with the US.

The strongest force in Iran is the Islamic Revolutionary Guard. It has enough fire power to stop oil tankers from traveling through the Straits of Hormuz carrying more than 70% of Middle East oil to Asia. Iran could as in the past easily put mines in passing oil tankers. It also have enough resources to fund Yemen to attack Saudi Arabia's pipeline.

It's because of this that President Trump does not want to escalate the war with Iran further.

The military move by Trump has provoked a global pushback

from the other five signatories of the Iran Nuclear Deal and other European countries including Belgium and Norway.

According to ***Rick Sanchez of RT News,*** in conversation with ***Rania Khalek, Host of The Now***, it appeared that General Solameini was on a peace mission with Pakistan and Iraq to work out a deal of cooperation between Iraq, Iran, and Saudi Arabia.

If this were to happen, then the US no longer has a chance of pitting one Arab country against another Arab country through fake news and propaganda. The US's influence in the Middle East would have been diminished.

The petrodollar deal that the US had with Saudi Arabia in the 1970s may be in jeopardy. It would immediately give China, Russia, India and many other countries an alternative to the petrodollar. This may cause a big drop in the US$. The US no longer has the unfair advantage of printing fiat money with impunity.

That could have been the reason why the US decided to kill this potential deal by killing Solameini to continue the hostilities and protect US interest there. If this is the truth, then President Trump, just like so many other politicians, had lied to the public.

War and oil are big businesses. They are breeding ground for corruption and assassination of those who threaten to disrupt these two businesses.

Iran nuclear deal framework

The Iran nuclear deal framework was a preliminary framework agreement reached in April 2015 between Iran and five members of the UN Security Council and the European Union (P5 + 1).

So the signatories of the Iran nuclear deal framework are Iran, the US, Russia, France, China, and the European Union.

Under the framework, Iran will redesign, convert, and reduce its nuclear facilities. In exchange, the US will lift trade sanctions against Iran and unfreeze Iranian assets held in foreign banks.

Iran knows about the issue of the hidden agenda of the US deep state. So understandably, Iran's President Hassan Rouhani welcomed the framework, but Iran's Supreme Leader, Ali Khamenei was less joyful, saying, "Nothing has happened yet."

Deep state

Every country has an intelligence agency. It is a government agency that is responsible for the collection, analysis, and exploitation of information in support of law enforcement, national security, military and foreign policy objectives.

Because of this secretive mission, it can become a very powerful but invisible force for or against the government.

The means of gathering information (data) are both overt (publicly open) or covert (hidden). These means may include espionage, communication interception, cryptoanalysis, cooperation with other institution, and evaluation of all the data collected.

The work of an intelligence agency is crucial because it can give early warning of impending dangers inside the country or from outside the country.

A deep state is a state within a state. It comprises people with immense power because of their insider information, experience, wealth, and influence. They comprises billionaires, selected members of the ruling party, bureaucrats, technocrats, politicians, royalty, CEOs of corporations and state-owned enterprises, and so forth.

In his book, ***Deep State: Trump, the FBI, and the rule of law***, James B Steward spells out all the activities going on secretly. Just like corporations all over the world, the deep state has two sets of records - those private closed-door meetings, and those announcements given through the media for the public which is politically correct.

That's why you may occasionally spot conflicting reports coming from different sources.

In his book, ***The Plot to Attack Iran: how the CIA and the deep state have conspired to vilify Iran,*** Dan Kovalik gives a priceless trove of information that the world but especially the Americans should know about the real truth behind the hidden agenda of the deep state in the US.

The deep state forms the conclusion that it is easier to deal with a secular government than a religious one. When the Shah was president of Iran, the relationship between Iran and the US was working well. But when Iran reverted to become an Islamic state, then the deep state would like a regime change.

In his book, ***A Conflict of Visions: ideological origins of political struggles,*** Thomas Sowell explains that controversies in politics arise from many sources. But conflicts that endure for generations or for centuries show a consistent pattern.

There is a clash of two opposite visions about the nature of man. Issues as diverse as criminal justice, income distribution, or war and peace repeatedly show those with one vision lining up on one side and those with the other vision lining up on the opposite side.

One vision allows for negotiations and trade-offs based more on economic consideration while on the opposite side holds the vision based on religious faith and cultural consideration.

Keeping this rationale in mind, you will interpret media reports with a more astute eye. It follows therefore that when the US applies even more sanctions on Iran, its hidden (military) objective is to make the Iranian people suffer so much that they will cause a revolutionary regime change to a secular state.

For a further understanding of the US-Iran conflict, you may like to watch the following two YouTube videos by Patrick Bet-David. Bet-David, born October 1978, is an Assyrian-Armenian, from Tehran, Iran, now residing in Dallas Texas. His videos are always very methodical and educational:

- ***US Iran Conflict***
- ***US-Iran: WWIII or Regime Collapse***

Separation of religion and state

According to the Ahmadiyya Muslim Community's understanding of Islam, Islamic principles state that the politics of government should be separate from the doctrine of religion. Its origins came from the Constitution of Medina which states that equal religious and communal rights must be given to all ethnic groups such as Muslims, Jews, and pagans.

Article 6 of the constitution of the US states that "no religious test shall ever be required as a qualification to any office or public trust under the United States."

Religion deal with faith. A good government has a different objective - producing positive results for the people regardless of race, language or religion.

That's why wise people want to separate state and religion.

Act now on your beliefs

The world is in turmoil. War is big business and big profits.

Beneath the hostile messages traveling back and forth are the hidden agendas of globalists who don't need to be in the battlefields. They are plotting ways to generate cash flows. Insiders can time their buy, sell, or short orders in the oil, gold, and stock markets, making billions of dollars each month.

War is big business. Globalists are collecting profits while soldiers die on the battlefields.

Heighten tensions means more arms sales of fighter jets, each costing $100 million. Each tank costs $1 million, and each US soldier wears equipment totaling $10,000. Military contractors send mercenaries into battlefields, and soldiers die while the generals just give orders - except of course General Soleimani.

In the meantime, the poor and middle class in Iran, Iran, Syria, Saudi Arabia, the US, and many European countries are not having a good day.

You must vote wisely. Make sure you don't vote a warmonger or a greedy and corrupt person into power.

Decisions have the power to steer and change your life forever. Therefore, nothing affects the quality of your life than your ability to make the right decisions. All that you have achieved or failed to achieved can be traced back to the decisions you've made - on issues concerning your vote, health, wealth, relationships, and life purpose.

Change your beliefs, and you will change your principles, values, virtues, habits, attitudes, social skills, ethics, behavior and so forth.

In life there are no mistakes, only lessons. The secret to resilience, happiness and a less stressful success is to avoid focusing on stagnant traits. Instead, focus on adopting an active, growth-oriented and problem-solving approach to life, and enjoying the journey together with your loved ones.

Here are the beliefs of greatness that will empower you to enjoy the journey with your loved ones:

- That which is hateful to you, do not do to your fellow human beings. Any interpretation of scriptures that bred hatred or disdain for others - whatever their beliefs - is illegitimate. (Hillel)
- True religion is protecting the powerless - orphans, widows, homeless, migrant workers, disabled, and injured soldiers returning from an unnecessary war.
- Power without love is reckless and abusive. Love without power is sentimental and anemic. Power at its best is love implementing the demands of justice. Justice at its best is power correcting everything that stands against love. (Martin Luther King)
- That which matter most must never be at the mercy of things that matter least. (Goethe)
- Courage is not the absence of fear but rather the judgment that something is more important than fear. The brave may not live forever. But the cautious do not live at all. (Meg Cabot)
- So long as you open your heart to beauty, hope, cheer, courage and power, so long are you young. (Samuel Ulman). I know of no more encouraging fact than the unquestionable ability of man to elevate his life by conscious endeavor (Henry David Thoreau).
- We should encourage each other to follow the rules of considerate conduct such as think before we act, listen more, argue less, seek first to understand, think twice before asking favors, avoid shifting responsibility and blame, avoid jumping to conclusions, respect other's opinion, and enjoying the

journey with your loved ones.

- If you want to achieve what you've never achieved before, you have to grow to become what you've never become before. (Brian Tracy). Insanity is doing the same over and over again and expecting different results. No problem can be solved at the same level of consciousness that created it. (Albert Einstein)
- Success and cheerfulness in life are not the result of what we have but rather how we live. What we do with the things we already have now makes the biggest difference in the quality of our life. (Tony Robbins)
- Studies have shown that companies hire for attitude and train for skills. (Singapore Airlines).
- Humility is the beginning of wisdom. (Zen habits)
- A foolish definition of success is the attainment of a certain amount of money, power, and privilege. A wise definition of success is enjoying the journey of lifelong learning with your loved ones.
- All men are created equal, endowed with the unalienable rights to life, liberty and the pursuit of happiness. (US Declaration of Independence)
- The world will be safer and prosperous when all nations adhere to the principles of peaceful coexistence where there is mutual respect for each other's territorial sovereignty and the right to self-determination and non-interference. (China-India)
- Whether a cat is black or white makes no difference. A cat that catches mice is a good cat. Whether we label an ideology socialism, capitalism, communism, or authoritarianism makes no difference. A government that can provide affordable subsidized public housing, meaningful

jobs, efficient transport system, clean environment, fantastic schools, universal health care, recreation centers, and national security is a good government and should be given a strong mandate to govern. (Deng Xiaoping)

- Every nation must strive to avoid contracting the national disease of schizophrenia where there are two equally dominant sectarian political parties, bickering with each other like two juveniles. It is best if there is a political party that promote universal values that protect the rights of minorities so as to gain at least 70% of popular vote thus attaining a strong mandate to govern.
- Workers must enjoy democracy at the workplace where they have a say in the management of the company and reserve the right to buy the company if the owners decide to sell.
- All citizens must have a fair share in the prosperity of the nation. This can be achieved by practicing universal basic income (UBI) calculated as a small percentage of the living wage. UBI is able to soften the ills of neoliberalism by reducing the pain and frustration of the underprivileged who are the victims of the wealth gap between the rich and the poor. UBI is able to reduce the risk of violent civil unrest.
- Every citizen must be given universal healthcare.
- Every person has the right to demand privacy, especially when he or she has not committed any crime. (Edward Snowden)
- Every person has the right to choose his own way of life without being judged or criticized so long as he or she respects the rule of law. He can choose voluntary simplicity, country living, living off the grid, any profession, urban competition, climbing the corporate ladder, activism, the military, or politics.
- Whistleblowers should be protected by law when they ex-

pose the wrongdoings within the company or government.

Chapter six

PREDATORY CAPITALISM

What is a predator?

In zoology, a predator is an animal that habitually prey on other animals.

A prey is an animal hunted or seized for food, especially by a carnivorous animal. A tiger, for example is a predator that will pounce on a deer and start taking bites from his prey, and eat his prey up.

A prey is also a person or thing that falls victim to an enemy, a disease, or any adverse agency.

In his book, ***Confessions of an Economic Hit Man***, John Perkins show how he played a role of an economic hit man in the process of economic colonization of Third World countries. This is done on behalf of a cabal of corporations, banks, and the United States government.

Economic hit men are highly paid professionals. They cheat the citizens of countries around the world out of trillions of dollars. They funnel money from the World Bank, the US Agency for International Development (USAID), and other foreign "aid" organizations into the coffers of huge corporations and the pockets of a few wealthy families who control the natural resources of countries.

Economic hit men orchestrate the widening gap between the rich and the poor.

An economic hit man will, for example, go to a prime minister of a country with a wonderful plan to prosper his country. He will explain to him that his country's economy will be boosted by this $10 billion infrastructure project. Then the economic hit man will give a great presentation with maps, architectural drawings, financial reports in glossy brochures, technical assistance, and soft loans from the World Bank.

The economic hit man says that he has in one hand a few million dollars which he will transfer into the prime minister's bank account when he gets approval for the $10 billion infrastructure project. Otherwise, he may need to use his gun. To do that, an economic hit man has the backing of some military force such as the NSA.

In the 1970s, John Perkins worked as Chief Economist for the Boston strategic-consulting firm Chas T Main. According to him, he was screened for this job by the US National Security Agency (NSA).

Perkin's role as the Chief Economist of Chas T Main advised the World Bank, United Nations, IMF, US Treasury Department, Fortune 500 corporations, and countries in Africa, Asia, Latin America, and the Middle East. Perkins later left and founded his own energy company., doing basically the same thing - an economic hit man.

The tools of economic hit men are awesome professional credentials, connections with big banks, great presentation skills, fraudulent financial reports in glossy brochures, rigged elections, payoffs, kickbacks, blackmail, extortion, sex, and murder.

In his book, ***The Corporation: the pathological pursuit of profit and power,*** Joel Bakan shows how the corporation has grown to have enormous power to wield over people and societies, using economic hit men to coordinate with corrupt national leaders, Wall Street, and government officials.

Joel Bakan is professor of law at the University of British Columbia, Canada. He has cocreated a documentary film and TV mini-series Called ***The Corporation*** based on his book.

Go watch this YouTube video and get outraged.

Criminal enterprises

In her book, ***Black Edge***, Sheelah Kolhatkar reveals the inside information, dirty money, and the quest to bring down the most wanted man on Wall Street.

There is a powerful new class of billionaire financiers in the world, who use their phenomenal wealth to write their own rules and laws. Chief among them is Steve Cohen, who is a Wall Street legend.

Steve Cohen built his hedge fund into a $15 billion empire. The FBI was investigating Cohen's firm SAC Capital for illegal insider information which gave him that black edge to beat his competitors.

SAC was found guilty of illegal insider trading and was fined $2 billion. Even though SAC Capital was fined, Cohen can continue to trade publicly from January 2018.

In 2015, US prosecutors were investing price fixing in currency market. They discovered that a dozen traders in JP Morgan were involved. Two traders pleaded guilty and were helping in the investigation. JP Morgan and one of its traders pleaded guilty.

After the 2008 crash, US prosecutors were investigating JP Morgan's global precious metal trading operation. They found that there was a conspiracy to conduct the affairs of an enterprise involved in interstate or foreign commerce through a pattern of racketeering activity.

This illegal conduct was widespread on the desk. These traders were engaged in thousands of episodes over an eight-year period. This was precisely the kind of conduct that the RICO statute was meant to punish.

RICO refers to the Racketeer Influenced and Corrupt Organizations Act, a law that is often used against organized crime rings.

US prosecutors charge the head of JP Morgan's global precious metal trading operation and two others under the RICO Act. This would mean that JP Morgan would be in deeper jeopardy as the investigation proceeds further.

US prosecutors charged that the head of the bank's precious metal desk, Michael Nowak, 45, Gregg Smith, 55, and Christopher Jordan, 47, ripped off market participants and even clients as they illegally moved prices for gold, silver, platinum, and palladium.

Richard Bowen

Richard Bowen was senior underwriter who oversaw 220 underwriters in Citigroup's consumer lending group. The job of underwriters was to trade loans. Bowen's job was to make sure that such loans meet Citigroup credit standards.

Bowen discovered that more than 60% of these home loans were defective. Bowen warned the banks' senior executives of problems with most of the prime mortgages it sold to Fannie Mae, Freddie Mac and other investors beginning 2006.

Bowen continued to warn Citigroup management about the risks to shareholders by the increasing defective rate of mortgages, which rose to 80% defective. But Citigroup management continued to purchase and sell increasing volumes of such products.

Bowen noticed, to his horror, that loans that were at first rejected were reversed and approved by Citigroup top managers. On November 7, 2007, he sent an email, headlined his email: URGENT - READ IMMEDIATELY - FINANCIAL ISSUES, to the following executives:

- Robert Rubin, Chairman of the executive committee of Citigroup's board of director
- Gary Crittenden, Chief Financial Officer
- David Bushnell, Senior Risk Officer
- Bonnie Howard, Chief Auditor

Bowen wrote:

"The reason for this urgent email concerns breakdowns of internal controls and resulting significant but possibly unrecognized financial losses existing within our organization."

Bowen recommended that senior management should start an investigation to be conducted by officers of the company outside of the Consumer Lending Group.

Citigroup spokeswoman Shannon Bell related that the issues raised by Mr. Bowen were promptly and carefully reviewed when he raised them and corrective actions were taken.

When the market crashed in 2008, the Financial Crisis Inquiry Commission called the top executives of Citigroup including Robert Bowen to testify before the commission.

The commission reached the conclusion that the bank cared very little about its underwriting standards even as a massive credit crisis was looming.

Eileen Foster

Eileen Foster was Senior Executive at Countrywide Financial Inc. She was in charge of monitoring and investigating possible fraud.

Foster found evidence of widespread mortgage fraud during an investigation in the Boston office. It soon became clear that this fraud was systemic. The loan officers received bonuses, and commissions for loans approved regardless of creditworthiness. It was an unwritten company policy to generate such behavior in its loan officers.

Recycle bins were filled with documents where signatures were cut off and pasted in other loan application forms, The recycle bins were filled with all sorts of photocopies that were tampered with.

When the market crashed in 2008, the Bank of America bought Countrywide Financial for pennies on the dollar. Foster was promoted at Bank of America.

However, when Foster was going to talk to government regulators, Bank of America fired her. Massachusetts's Attorney General Martha Coakley sued the Bank of America, JP Morgan, Wells Fargo, Citigroup, and Ally Financial for their role in the foreclosure mess.

Eileen Foster, as a whistleblower received $1 million.

Edward O'Donnel, a former Countrywide executive, had even more information on the fraud committed, O'Donell brought a suit against Bank of America on behalf of the US government.

At the end of the trial, US District Judge Jed Rakoff in Manhattan gave the verdict that Bank of America was liable for the sale of questionable loans to Fannie Mae and Freddie Mac before the

2008 financial crisis. Bank of America was ordered to pay a penalty of $1.7 billion. O'Donell would get a share on its recovery.

Tyler Schultz

In October 2015, the Inc magazine featured Elizabeth Holmes a young blonde woman wearing a black turtleneck on its cover. She was Elizabeth Holmes, the founder of Theranos. Theranos promised to revolutionize blood testing as the world knew it. She was promoted as "the next Steve Jobs."

Former US Secretary of the Treasury George Schultz, was an early investor and a member of the Board of Directors of Theranos from 2011 to 2015.

Tyler Schultz first met Elizabeth Holmes in his grandpa's living room. When he heard about this wonderful company. He wanted to invest right away, and he did. Many investors rushed into invest in Theranos as well. Total investment was $700 million.

Tyler Schultz was employed by Theranos. Even on the first day, Schultz noticed many strange things. The work culture was toxic. People who spoke up were fired on the spot. So most employees didn't say anything and kept their heads down.

Six months into his his employment, Schultz raised a couple of concerns with Holmes. Lab tests were showing high failure rates. Holmes assured Schultz that everything was fine. These lab results were not interpreted correctly.

These lab tests were for serious diseases. Schultz felt that this was serious - people were going to get hurt. So Schultz sent an anonymous tip to the new York state public health lab. But Schultz didn't receive any reply. Then he received a message from John Carryrou a health care fraud reporter for the Wall Street Journal.

A month after this, Tyler went over to visit his parents. His dad was furious with him. His grandpa called and asked for Tyler to come to the phone. Grandpa George said, "Elizabeth's been telling me you're giving away trade secrets to Wall Street Journal."

Schultz's family assured Tyler that Theranos just needed Tyler to meet with Theranos' lawyers and sign a one-page non-disclosure agreement and the issues would go away.

Tyler got a shock when Theranos's lawyers came from a back room and gave him many legal forms to sign including a restraining order. Tyler's parents begged him to sign these legal papers.

Tyler refused to budge as he wanted to remain true to his values.

In the end, the court ordered Theranos to shut down. Elizabeth Holmes and Balwani were charged with two counts of conspiracy to commit wire fraud and nine counts of wire fraud. They each faced a maximum of 20 years in prison and up to $2.7 million in fines.

Tyler Schultz was awarded the Cliff Robertson Sentinel Award for choosing truth over self.

Office of the whistleblower

The US Securities and Exchange Commission (SEC) is the office where whistleblower can report possible securities law violations. Assistance and information from a whistleblower can be among the most powerful weapons in the law enforcement arsenal of the SEC.

Whistleblowers can provide the circumstances and individuals involved that would greatly assit SEC in identifying possible fraud and other violations much earlier than might otherwise have been possible.

Whistleblowers can help the SEC to minimize the harm to investors, better preserve the integrity of the US capital markets, and more swiftly hold accountable those responsible for unlawful conduct.

The SEC is authorized by Congress to provide rewards to whistleblowers for tips that result in enforcement actions taken by the SEC. The range of awards ranges from 10% to 30% of the money collected. More than $300 million have so far been awarded to whistleblowers. Whistleblowers are protected under the Dodd Frank Wall Street Reform and Consumer Protection Act (Dodd-Frank Act) of 2010.

Financial fraud takes many forms. Publicly traded companies report major events to the public through press releases on line and through Form 8-K which is filed with the SEC. They may contain fraudulent information - of overstating their profitability or failing to report a significant liability.

You can reach the Office of the Whistleblower at (202) 551-4790 and (703) 813-9322 by Fax.

You can contact the SEC at:

100 F Street NE
Mail Stop 5631
Washington DC 20549
USA

Tactics

One of the ways to thrive in a broken financial system is to be knowledgeable in the world of success and finance.

Edward de Bono is widely regarded as the leading authority in the direct teaching of thinking as a skill. He has written more than 62 books which have been translated into 37 languages.

He had two television series and there are more than 4 million references to his works in the Internet. He is the author of ***Six Thinking Hats.***

In his book, ***Tactics****, the art and science of success*, Edward de Bono provides the answers to these three questions:

- What do the successful have in common?
- Are the qualities one expect to find in the chairmen and CEOs of powerful corporations the same qualities that have helped them climb to the top?
- How are those same CEOs similar in style and demeanor to, say, a prolific novelist, or a rock star?

Edward de Bono looks at the thoughts, the techniques, even the strategies of thinking among some of the most commercially and artistically successful people in America and the United Kingdom.

Edward de Bono gathers a cross-section of people who talking about the various elements of their success:

- Jackie Steward - the greatest motor racing champion of all time
- Roy Cohn - toughest lawyer
- Diane von Furstenberg - fashion tycoon
- Norman Lear - top television producer
- Sting - a pop star
- Harry Helmsley - the world's greatest hotelier
- Malcolm Forbes - a millionaire publisher
- Paul MacCready - the inventor of man-powered flight.

Edward de Bono interviewed them and discovered that they are either lucky, mad, or highly talented. De Bono further asks:

- Are these people risk takers?
- What are their background influences?
- How do they deal with other people, with negotiation, with their own expectations of themselves and the people they work with?

What Edward de Bono hope you the reader would respond is:

Why not me?

At no point in his book did Edward de Bono try to define success. It can be so varied, as you can see. But the basic definition is that success is to set out to do something and to succeed in doing it.

There is one thing that Edward de Bono did not talk about in his book, and that is find out what are the endings like for these successful people. The bad news in that more than 30% of them lost all their money, had bad health, and died lonely.

So Stephen Covey's 2nd habit is a gem of wisdom - Begin with the end in mind.

Know thyself. Know thy enemies

Most people think they know their enemies. But not really.

We are our own worst enemy.

What?

Sometimes, we think our best friend, sibling, or boss betrayed us. Yes. But it is only partly true. Most of the time, we should take at least 60% of the blame.

Ask yourself:

Why should we allow ourselves to be betrayed and cheated by others?

We don't know ourselves well enough. We may be too self-righteous. We may have a distorted self-image. We don't know where we have competitive advantage, and where we are simply hopeless in a doing a particular task.

Studies reveal that most people hate their jobs, family, religion, and country.
This is because we have a distorted self-image, making all the wrong decisions in our vote, health, wealth, relationship, and life purpose. We are full of regrets and are still hanging on to the hurt.

We say YES when we wanted to say NO.

So what shall we do?

Know thyself!

Here are a few ways to know yourself more thoroughly.

In his book, ***Color Code***, Taylor Hartman shows you a new way of seeing yourself, your relationship, and life.

Our personality has already been hardwired at birth. We may mitigate our weaknesses over time, but they are still there.

Human beings have four motivations present in different proportions - power, altruism, peace, and fun.

All four motivations are important. That is why when you rely only on yourself, you will eventually fail. It is best if you have an A-team that has a rich mix of personality types to produce creative cooperation, SYNERGY, and sustainability.

Rotary International is a good example of SYNERGY. Local groups are made up of people from all sectors of the economy so that their proposals are always rock solid.

When doctors, soldiers, teachers, athletes, businessmen, engineers, singers, and politicians can listen to each other, we'll have a better world.

If you want to have a strengths and weakness analysis, check out this website:

https://www.123test.com/strengths-weaknesses-analysis.

Last but not least, watch this YouTube video:

Are you difficult to love?

We are insufferable when we don't even consider a small possibility that we may be a difficult person to love.

Almost all of us are tricky characters.

Watch this YouTube video, become more self-aware, and see yourself blossom. This YouTube video from ***The School of Life*** will work like a mirror where we will see our good traits and our horrible ones.

12 bad habits

Whatever your profession is, be aware of the 12 bad habits that hold good people back. Break these bad habits before they break you.

Most people learn their biggest lessons from their mistakes.

There are a million ways to be succeed on your own terms. But career experts will tell you that there are only a handful of bad habits that will crash your career.

James Waldroop and Timothy Butler are directors of MBA career development at the Harvard Business School. They are the creators of the Internet-based interactive career-assessment program CareerLeader, currently used by over 100 corporations and MBA programs worldwide.

Waldroop & Butler are leaders in the area of executive coaching and intervention. They have consulted with many of the top corporations.

In their book, ***Maximum Success: changing the 12 behavior patterns that keep you from getting ahead,*** Waldroop & Butler lists down the 12 bad habits that can hamstring your career success and your financial future:

- Never feeling good enough
- Seeing the world in black and white
- Doing too much, pushing to hard
- Avoiding conflict at any cost
- Running roughshod over the opposition
- Rebel looking for a cause
- Always swinging for the fence
- When fear is in the driver's seat
- Emotionally tone-deaf
- When no job is good enough
- Losing the path

These bad habits do not appear at random. They emanate from four unresolved psychological issues:

- Distorted self-image
- Not taking others' perspective

- Not coming to terms with authority
- Using power without finesse

Study these concepts and see your career soar.

The Power of Full Engagement

Jim Loehr and Tony Schwartz are senior partners and principals at LGE Performance Systems. They developed the Full Engagement model and the Corporate Athlete Training System. Each of them have worked with senior executives and managers.

We live in a digital world. This means that things are happening fast and furious. Facing crushing workloads, we try to cram as much as we can every day. We try to manage time and that's a big mistake.

In their book, ***The Power of Full Engagement,*** Loehr & Schwartz reveals that managing ENERGY, not time, is the key to high performance and personal renewal.

Leaders are the steward of organizational energy - in organizations and even in families. Each of us have hour dimensions - body, emotions, mind, and spirit. All four dimensions must be fully fired up if we want peak performance.

We must learn how to be physically energized, emotionally connected, mentally focused, and spiritually aligned with our values. This is how we wake up eager to go to work.

Less than 30% of the work force are fully engaged in their work. Our performance, health, and happiness are grounded in the skillful management of our ENERGY. The power of full engagement is based on these four principles of managing energy:

- Full engagement requires drawing on four separate but related sources of energy: physical, emotional, mental, and spiritual.
- Because energy capacity diminishes both with overuse and with underuse, we must balance energy expenditure with intermittent energy renewal.
- To build capacity, we must push beyond our normal limits, training in the same systematic way that elite athletes do.
- Positive energy rituals - highly specific routines for managing ENERGY - are the key to full engagement and sustained high performance.

Multiple streams of income

There are many ways to achieve financial security. Usually it is through having multiple streams of income. So when you retire from your full-time job, the other streams of income will continue to provide your monthly cash flow.

In his book, ***Multiple Streams of Income: how to generate a lifetime of unlimited wealth,*** Robert G Allen shows how you can learn about 10 revolutionary ways to generate over $100,000 a year, especially in the United States.

Allen is the author of New York Times #1 bestsellers ***Nothing Down*** and ***Creating Wealth***.

Allen has researched hundreds of income-producing opportunities and narrowed them down to **10 surefire moneymakers for the new millennium**:

- How to retire wealthy on a dollar a day
- How to earn an extra million in your lifetime

- The 9 characteristics of the ideal home-based business
- Low-risk ways to double your money in the stock market - FAST
- How to earn 18%, 36%, and up to 50% returns on your investment - guaranteed
- How to earn as much as $1000 a day right from your own home
- How to profit from the Internet explosion
- How to become an information multimillionaire
- How to cash in on the secrets of intellectual property
- And much, much more.

The business of life

Now, let's talk about Warren Buffet.

Warren Buffet is one of the most respected men in the world. In other words, he is respected not just because he had billions of dollars to his name. Many dictators have this kind of money too.

Buffet is respected because he wants to prove to himself that ***nice guys can finish first.***

The secret of success is to focus on one thing where you have competitive advantage. If you don't have competitive, don't compete. It is better to dig just one well 100 feet deep than to dig ten wells ten feet deep. The keyword is FOCUS.

Many rich people are like the hare in Aesop's Fables. They impress others on how hard they work and how aggressive they are as taskmasters. But not Warren Buffet. He is more like the tortoise out to prove to the hare who laughed at him that "slow and steady wins the race." He treats his managers like business partners.

Alice Schroeder was an insurance industry analyst and a gifted writer. She is known for her keen perception and business acumen. Buffet was impressed by her writing. When they met, Schroeder suggested that while the world knows about Buffet's investing prowess, the world didn't know much about him as a person.

Warren Buffet decided to cooperate with Alice Schroeder on a book about him that he himself would not have written. The result is the book titled: ***The Snowball:*** *Warren Buffet and the Business of Life.*

This also illustrate the power of synergy - creative cooperation!

This book is more valuable than other investment books because it talks about the business of life. Investing is easy to understand but difficult to apply because of the business of life - there are many distractions and bad habits in life. We are all tricky characters.

This book explores Warren Buffet's larger philosophy which is bound in a complex personality.

Just like what Edward de Bono try to uncover, background influences playing a part in the ease or difficulty in succeeding.

Warren's grandpa owned a grocery store in Omaha, Nebraska, USA. Warren's dad, Howard Buffet was a member of the US House of Representatives from Nebraska's 2nd precinct. Howard embraced Christian ideals, being active members of Dundee Presbyterian Church.

Howard Buffet started a small stock brokerage firm. Warren was born with business in his blood. He purchased his first stock when he was 11 years old. He worked in his family's grocery store in Omaha. Warren spent his days watching what investors were doing and listening to what they say.

As a teenager, Warren took odd jobs, from washing cars to delivering papers. He used his savings to purchase pinball machines that he placed in local businesses.

Warren wanted to do business instead of going to college. But his dad pressed him to attend the University of Pennsylvania. He transferred to the University of Nebraska soon after.

After graduating from the University of Nebraska, Warren proceeded to study at Columbia Business School. There he studied under Benjamin Graham and David Dodd. Warren developed the proper intellectual framework and a road map for investing from Benjamin Graham's book, ***The Intelligent Investor*** and ***Security Analysis*** by Benjamin Graham and David Dodd.

Warren admitted that he was 85% Graham. Graham always looked for undervalued stocks. While Warren also looked at stocks from this angle, his greater emphasis, unlike Graham, is that he looked at the stock from the angle of a business with all its components - products, management, longevity of the business and so forth. Is this business a strong enterprise worth owning long term?

Warren likes to use the analogy of baseball. In baseball, you have to hit at every ball pitched at you. Warren's method is the opposite of baseball. Warren prefers to wait and wait until he could hit a home run.

So in a way, Graham's method is more friendly to the average investor, whereas Warren's method requires a more thorough look at stocks as businesses, and to buy only when the timing is perfectly right. This is more like the contrarian method of investing.

Here are eight tips from Warren Buffet:

- **Business.** The basic ideas of investing are to look at stocks as business, use the market's fluctuations to your advantage, and seek a margin of safety. That's what Ben Graham taught us. A hundred years from now, they will still be the cornerstones of investing.
- **Communicate well**. If you want to manage a fund and get people interested in your ideas, the ability to communicate well with your investors is crucial.
- **Read widely**. To make the right decisions in investing, you need to read widely, not just books, but articles, breaking news and so forth - maybe up to 500 pages a day.
- **Choose your friends wisely.** Warren's friendship with Benjamin Graham, David Dodd, and Charlie Munger certainly helped him to succeed.
- **Kill busy work.** Buffet says NO to almost everything. He eliminated almost all the obligatory CEO tasks from his schedule. He seldom talk to analysts, or the media, don't attend industry events and seldom attend internal meetings.
- **Simplify.** Always keep things super simple. He cuts out most of the bureaucracy in his company. Simplicity is also translated into frugality. He lives in the same house he bought more than 60 years ago.
- **Focus.** He focuses on a few high-quality bets and keep it for decades.
- **Avoid the technology band wagon.** Equipment may not necessarily make you a better investor, especially if you only want just a few high-quality bets.

Financial discipline

Success is a horrible teacher. You learn best from your failures and mistakes so that you can learn your lessons in a painful way - once bitten twice shy.

But there is an even better way.

Why should you go through the pain when you can choose to learn from other people's mistakes, losses, and successes. You don't have to reinvent the wheel all over again.

In her blog, ***The Money Habit***, a woman that goes by her pen name J P Livingston shares her story.

After 7 years of working at an investment firm in New York City, J P Livingston had built a $2.25 million nest egg, enough to quit her job and retire at age 28.

Livingston was able to do that thanks to a series of raises, and then developing a savings rate of 70%. Her wise investing help her make a small fortune.

If you can't save at 70%, a 35% savings rate will still get you there.

As you can see, anyone can take these three steps to achieve financial freedom earlier:

- Increase your savings rate through wise spending and wise frugal living, while you are still young and optimistic. Use Warren Buffet's frugal living as a great example.
- Expand your earning power by upgrading your high-value marketable skills.
- Intelligent investing the Ben Graham-Warren Buffet way.

The earlier you implement the above discipline, the more will your money work for you through compound interest.

Remember this: No pain, no gain. No drill, no skill.

Saving money is building a machine that works for you while you sleep, eat, travel, and retire.

One more great incentive in wealth accumulation is this: With wealth comes a reputation for wisdom, prudence, self-confidence, courage, greatness, and other unearned virtues.

Here is an example of ***how delaying gratification for 8 years early in life*** will put you ahead of someone who start saving 8 years later.

Tom starts saving $300 a month for 8 years at age 19 until he is 27 years old. At a compound interest of 10%, his savings of around $28,800 grew to $1.9 million by age 60 even though Tom stop saving at age 27.

Jerry starts saving $300 per month only when he is 27 years old. Even if Jerry continue to save all the way to age 60, his savings amounts to $140,000. Yet his retirement fund of $1.6 million is less than Tom's retirement fund of $1.9 million.

The big difference is just eight years of delaying gratification when Tom was just 19 years old. You are then set for life.

That's the power of compound interest at 10% per year. This rate is achievable. But even at say 5%, the basic arithmetics still work out the same.

Don't be insulted when someone says, "If you are so smart, why aren't you rich?"

Being smart and well-educated is not enough. You have to be frugal, prudent and shrewd in financial matters.

Why not take the pain before pleasure to reap the reward of financial freedom.

Remember this:

With wealth comes a reputation for wisdom, prudence, self-confidence, courage, greatness and other unearned virtues.

The reward of a brighter future is worth a little discipline in your early years.

6 money traps

The above illustration can be distorted by the following 6 money traps that you must avoid especially in your early 30s when your youthful exuberance is at its peak:

- **Buying an expensive new car.** A car has one of the highest rate of depreciation. By the end of the first year, a new car will lose 30% of its purchase price. At the end of the third year, a new car would lose roughly half its price, even though it may still look awesome. So why not buy a 3-year-old awesome looking car at half the price?
- **Buying an expensive house.** People in the real estate business have tight connections with banks. They may sweet-talk you into buying a bigger house. The higher the price tag, the higher commission the real estate agent will make. If you have only $30,000, how can you buy that $500,000 house? No problem. We can get you a $470,000 mortgage loan at 1% interest the first year. Don't ever fall for this. The loan agreement includes a clause that says that the interest is pegged to the interbank rate plus 3%. Do the opposite of what the bank want you to do - save towards having a big down payment .
- **Spending too much**. Work on a budget: E.g. Savings 35%, foods 35% transport 20% and so on. Failing to distinguish between needs and wants make many people poor. As Warren Buffet says, "Buying things you don't need may lead to selling things you do need."

- **Having a high maintenance significant other**. Choose your friends carefully. Frugality is a virtue. Money is the number one source of conflict. Prequalify your friends based on the virtue of wise and frugal living. Befriend principle-centered people.
- **Paying too much on your credit card.** 2% a month seems like a small amount. But if you have balances, the annual rate is 24%. Banks know your weaknesses and will pander to your baser instincts. Don't fall for it. Pay off your balances every single month, unless you have valid reasons why you aren't doing it.
- **Not investing.** Money shrinks in value due to inflation. In fact, inflation is an economic policy of government so that the economy has the incentives for the active players to continue participating. So you must invest and invest wisely. Intelligent investing keeps you afloat no matter how high the tide is.

Go watch this YouTube and get inspired:

6 Money Traps To Avoid In Your 30s by Mark Moss

Distributed ledger technology

In the 2019 Spring Meetings of the World Bank Group and the IMF in Washington DC, IMF Chief Christine Lagarde said that block chain innovators are shaking the traditional financial world. They will disrupt the activities of incumbent players.

Several big players like JP Morgan and Facebook are launching their own digital coins. Regulators and central banks are receptive to this trend. New inventions using distributed ledger technology will have a positive effect on the business model of commercial banks.

Crypto markets need to be regulated by the same laws that apply to the traditional banking sector in order to protect consumers and safeguard systemic stability.

What is a distributed ledger?

A distributed ledger is a data base that exists across many locations and among many participants. It is superior to a centralized ledger which has a fixed central location. So when it fails, the whole system will stop functioning.

So a distributed ledge is decentralized to eliminate the need for a central authority or intermediary to process, validate or authenticate transaction. When consensus is reached by the parties involved, the transaction is time-stamped and given a unique cryptographic signature. Records of such transactions are open for viewing. All these transactions will be lightning fast using AI computing power.

The technology provides a verifiable and auditable history of all information stored in that particular data-set. Block-chain is a type of distributed ledger, using blocks of data. So unlike traditional banking, block-chain and distributed ledger do no require a centralized clearing house. They provide an accurate and immutable audit trail, and they are transparent, open to public viewing.

Rumors has it that the globalists are planning a new world order where neither the US$ nor the Chinese yuan would be the preeminent reserve currency. They will be replaced by distributed ledger technology to be used as IMF Special Drawing Rights (SDRs).

Therefore, if the world seeks to diversify away from the US$, then the IMF can use distributed ledger technology to create the SDRs as the global currency accepted by all nations.

If distributed ledger technology is implemented by major

countries, then it will disrupt the world financial system as we know it. The US can no longer print fiat money without negative consequences.

China, Russia, India, Japan, South Korea, the European Union countries, UK, Iran, Turkey, Iraq, Saudi Arabia, Brazil, South Africa and many other countries can all dump the US$ to buy these new SDRs. There is less need to buy US Treasury bills. The US$ may nose-dive, and inflation will soar.

Should such a plan be launched, then the US can no longer use sanctions to bully the other nations like Iran and Iraq. The US financial system will be disrupted, and the US can no longer have such a huge military budget to wage regime change wars. There will be more creative cooperation among the Middle East countries, and the world will be more stable and peaceful.

The Palestine will get a fairer settlement of the conflict with Israel without the help of the US.

When all of the above takes place, there will be many opportunities for YOU to make a fortune - such as shorting the US$, buying gold, and buying stocks at the bottom of a global market crash and recession.

Bloomberg News

Bloomberg News states that the double-digits return of 2019 will be hard to repeat for year 2020. Investors will earn a lot less.

Bloomberg News is back with its reader's digest of research notes for year 2020 from the biggest financial institutions:

- **Base case.** The trade war remains at the core of our macro forecasts, with some attention focused on the 2020 US presidential elections. We expect a higher bond yield in the US market and a softer dollar in both G10 and the emerging markets (EM).

- **Growth.** Growth should re-assert its dominance over value in a modest economic growth scenario with low interest rates. Cyclicals are still very cheap relative to bond-like defensives and some further valuation adjustment could take place.

- **Recession.** Governments may be able to avert a global recession. If this is so, the outlook for commodities remains benign. Gold will continue to be seen as a powerful hedge against geopolitical risks.

- **Monetary policy.** Significant monetary easing by central banks should support growth at low but positive levels. We expect the US Federal Reserve rate cut to come in the first half of 2020. Central banks in other countries will most probably follow suit.

- **Negative rates.** The hunt for yield will remain a key theme in the era of ultra low interest rates. Fixed income returns may be lower in 2020 than in 2019. Fixed income assets in Japan and the EU look the most risky.

- **Inflation.** US Treasuries maintain their ballast properties against equity selloffs. It's time to rethink the role of government bonds outside the US. Secular stagnation with low growth, weak inflation and low interest rates is likely to define global economy for the next five years.

- **Fiscal policy.** Income and opportunities from rotation towards neglected areas will be the equity 2020 story. The lack of directional trends in the markets, and weak earnings growth should drive investors to search for areas of resilience in the equity/dividend space.

- **US Elections.** There could clearly be some headline risks for stocks once there is clarity on the Democratic nominee. The equity volatility markets are implying a 1.5% move in broad stock indexes around Super Tuesday (March 6, 2020), when a large number of Democratic primaries are held, and a 3% move on the day of the general elections.

- **Politics.** Lingering political uncertainty will create persistent direct and sentiment-driven drags on global trade, business investment and services. US-China trade tensions remain a key risk and we do not foresee a quick resolution. Korea and Taiwan are vulnerable to trade conflict centered on the technology sector. The dispute between Japan and Korea will further disrupt the global tech supply chain.
- **Trade.** New themes will emerge in emerging markets from a more fragmented world and a retreat in global trade. Investors will have to go beyond the traditional "global" emerging market concept and dig deeper to capture attractive opportunities and theme.
- **Volatility.** We should not rule out possible bouts of bond market volatility. Given the low-yield environment, we favor strategies that limit volatility, focus on income returns and/or are diversified and flexible enough to generate steady returns through active allocation.
- **Brexit.** The dollar will gradually deflate over the course of 2020 as US-China tensions moderate, hard Brexit risks diminish, and global growth picks up. Towards the end of 2020, escalating US political risk could deal a more severe blow. But we need to get much closer to the Presidential election before the FX consequences are felt.

Preparing for a market crash

There is a higher probability of a market crash this year (2020) than last year.

Red-flagging is very important in gathering information about intelligent investing.

What is a red flag?

Red flag as a transitive verb means to identify or draw attention to (a problem or an issue to be dealt with)

Red flag as a noun means a warning signal or sign.

For example, when a YouTube video shows an investment advisor recommending a stock to buy, and he does not state exactly when he made this recommendation, this is a red flag that this advisor is either careless, incompetent, or fraudulent.

Why do you say that? you may ask.

This is because the state of the stock market changes every minute, hour and day. What was a good recommendation of buying ABC stock at $77 three years ago is now very risky at $210. There is less margin of safety at $210 than at $77.

Despite diplomacy, collective expertise, and experience, history continues to repeat itself, not exactly but generally. A bullish period of irrational exuberance in markets is always followed by an equally irrational period of despair and chaos. To be a great investor, you must be fearful when too many people are optimistic, and buy when almost everyone is extremely pessimistic.

In the 1970s, cheap foreign aid poured into Latin America, especially to Mexico, Brazil, and Argentina. Then it crashed in **1982** and the IMF had to bail these countries out.

The savings and loans crisis caused the market to crash in **1987**. This caused riots to break out in many countries including China.

In **1991**, the Soviet Union collapsed.

Mexico suddenly devalued its Mexican peso to caused the Tequila crisis and the market collapsed in **1994**.

The devaluation of the Thai baht caused the Asian financial crisis in **1997.**

The dot.com bull run in the technology sector came to an abrupt end in **1999.**

On September 11, **2001**, terrorist hijacked four planes to crash into the World Trade Center in New York and the Pentagon building

On February 27, **2004**, Abu Sayyaff sank the super ferry in Philippines.

The US housing market collapse that almost collapsed the entire US financial system in **2008.** It was caused by the biggest bankruptcies in financial history. It caused the loss of 30 million jobs. Millions lost their homes. Trillions of wealth were wiped out. It almost collapsed the financial systems of several countries.

In **2017**, housing speculation in Xiong-an, China caused housing prices to double overnight. 50% of online purchases took place in China.

Crisis fears rise as global debt hit a record $250 trillion caused by central bank lowering interest rates to near zero and corporations buybacks.

What's going to happen now?

Rebalance your financial portfolio

Our world may be described as volatile, uncertain, complex, ambiguous, dangerous, and highly competitive.

Instead of trying to speculate, forecast, and pick the lottery winner, it is better to invest with the objective of hedging against measurable risks. Measurability is important in intelligent investing.

Divide your financial resources into five categories, and using your experience and common sense (thinking before you act), rebalance your portfolio after every disruption in the market. This is done to return your portfolio to its fundamentally strong proportions:

- **Your high-value skills (1%)** - this is the most ignored and forgotten asset. Your improving mindset is your biggest asset. If you have just $1,000 for investing, invest in your high-value skills - take an investing the Warren Buffet way online course, buy a powerful self-improvement book, enhance your social and copywriting skills, buy lunch for someone who can teach you one skill, give you one tip, bribe your mentor, befriend your bank manager, and so forth.
- **Insurance (6%)** - hedging with options, gold, silver, futures, maybe crypto-currency.
- **Cash (10%)** - some low-risk treasury bills and bonds (do not ignore country risk)
- **Growth (38%)** - a few great companies showing capital gains through thick and thin (do not ignore country risk; use leverage in a young bull market)
- **Income (45%)** - a few great companies paying high dividend for the last 20 years and/or a rental property that has a high net yield with potential for future growth. (do not ignore country risk; use leverage in a young bull market)

For example, let's say you made a killing in a put option. Add the profits to your total portfolio value, and rebalance your portfolio back to your base proportions. You can adjust it to suit the size of your portfolio and your experience. But the relative sizes must be kept - meaning that the higher the risks, the smaller should be its proportion in your portfolio.

You are your best financial advisor - your most valuable asset is YOU! Invest in your training first. Stay away from active hedge funds. They generate fees for themselves with their over-complicated portfolio and algorithms to impress and confuse you. They seldom beat the passive index funds. Why pay their salaries?

Does this make sense to you?

Investment Plan B

However there is one big catch. Many of the great gains by all the well-known stocks like Apple, Amazon, Google, and Facebook are big-cap stocks powered by the China Factor.

So the biggest question has not been answered yet:

Will the Chinese economy falter or even collapse?

So you need to have a PLAN B.

For me, I will choose to follow or at least listen to Matt McCall. He left Wall Street to focus mainly on micro-cap stocks, those stocks with a capitalization of less than $2 billion. Because of their huge capitalization, gains on blue chips are steady but not spectacular. But gains on microcaps can be truly awesome. It's like buying Amazon in the 1980s when people were laughing at Jeff Bezos.

You can find Matt McCall at InvestorPlace.com

Another hidden factor is the anticipation of the decline of the US$ due to the IMF launching a new type of SDR using distributed ledger technology.

Then there is a US presidential election coming up in November 2020.

Whether the Wuham health crisis may trigger a financial melt-down, no one can be absolutely sure.

So the next few months in 2020 are going to be really tricky.

Someday is a disease

So when are you going to implement all the financial ideas given?

Someday is a disease that will take your dreams to your grave with you.

Quoting Tim Ferriss, author of the best-selling *The 4-Hour Workweek*:

I once asked my mom how she decided to have her first child, little ol' me. The answer was simple: "It was something we wanted, and we decided there was no point in putting it off. The timing is never right to have a baby." And so it was.

For all the most important things, the timing always sucks. Waiting for a good time to quit your job? The stars will never align and the traffic lights of life will never all be green at the same time. The universe doesn't conspire against you, but it doesn't go out of its way to line up the pins either. Conditions are never perfect. "Someday" is a disease that will take your dreams to the grave with you. Pros and cons lists are just as bad. If it's important to you and you want to do it "eventually," ***just do it and correct course along the way.***

Quoting ancient wisdom:

There is an appointed time for everything
And there is a time for every event under heaven.
A time to give birth and a time to die.
A time to plant and a time to uproot what is planted.
A time to kill and a time to heal.
A time to tear down and a time to build up.
A time to weep and a time to laugh.
A time to mourn and a time to dance.
A time to throw stones and a time to gather stones.
A time to embrace and a time to shun embracing.
A time to search and a time to give up as lost.
A time to keep and a time to throw away.
A time to tear apart and a time to sew together.
A time to be silent and a time to speak.
A time to love and a time to hate.
A time for war and a time for peace.

Look to this day
For it is life, the very life of life.
In its brief course lies all the verities
And realities of your existence:
The bliss of growth
The glory of action
The splendor of beauty.

For yesterday is but a dream
And tomorrow only a vision
BUT TODAY WELL-LIVED
Makes every yesterday a dream of happiness and
Every tomorrow a vision of hope.
Look well therefore to this day.
Such is the salutation to the Dawn.

Quoting William Shakespeare (Julius Caesar):

Cowards die many times before their deaths
The valiant never taste but once...
Men at some time are masters of their fate;
The fault lies, dear Brutus, not in our stars
But in ourselves, that we are underlings...

There is a tide in the affairs of men
Which taken at the flood leads on to fortune.
Omitted, all the voyage of their life
Is bound in shallows and in miseries.
On such a full sea are we afloat.
And we must take the current when it serves,
Or lose our ventures.

Act now on your beliefs

One of the ways to thrive in a broken financial system is to be knowledgeable in the world of success and finance. There are three big things you must do to ensure your financial security:

- Improve your earning power. Your most valuable asset is YOU! Achieve your best performance and personal renewal in your profession. You must deal with the 12 bad habits that hold you back - ***Maximum Success by James Waldroop & Timothy Butler.***

- Invest the Warren Buffet way with his biography as your handbook: ***The Snowball: Warren Buffet and the Business of Life*** by Alice Schroeder.

- **Master the contrarian approach** by shorting the US$, buy gold, and buy stocks when blood is on the street. The next financial crisis may be as bad as the 1929 Wall Street crash.

> Be prepared for a currency reset and a less military US. Be prepared for a world where all national currencies will be treated equally. The US$ nor the Chinese yuan will serve as a reserved currency. It will be an IMF SDR using a distributed ledge technology. It will be painful for those who are not prepared for this likely scenario.

Financial fraud takes many forms. You can do your part by reporting any wrongdoing to the anti-corruption agency in your country.

Publicly traded companies report major events to the public through press releases on line and by filing with the stock exchange commission of your country. In the US, companies have to file Form 8-K with the SEC. They may contain fraudulent information - of overstating their profitability or failing to report a significant liability.

For those in the US, you can reach the ***Office of the Whistleblower*** at (202) 551-4790 and (703) 813-9322 by Fax.

You can contact the SEC at:

100 F Street NE
Mail Stop 5631
Washington DC 20549
USA

Decisions have the power to steer and change your life forever. Therefore, nothing affects the quality of your life than your ability to make the right decisions. All that you have achieved or failed to achieved can be traced back to the decisions you've made - on issues concerning your vote, health, wealth, relationships, and life purpose.

Change your beliefs, and you will change your principles, values, virtues, habits, attitudes, social skills, ethics, behavior and so forth.

In life there are no mistakes, only lessons. The secret to resilience, happiness and a less stressful success is to avoid focusing on stagnant traits. Instead, focus on adopting an active, growth-oriented and problem-solving approach to life, and enjoying the journey together with your loved ones.

Here are the beliefs of greatness that will empower you to enjoy the journey with your loved ones:

- That which is hateful to you, do not do to your fellow human beings. Any interpretation of scriptures that bred hatred or disdain for others - whatever their beliefs - is illegitimate. (Hillel)
- True religion is protecting the powerless - orphans, widows, homeless, migrant workers, disabled, and injured soldiers returning from an unnecessary war.
- Power without love is reckless and abusive. Love without power is sentimental and anemic. Power at its best is love implementing the demands of justice. Justice at its best is power correcting everything that stands against love. (Martin Luther King)
- That which matter most must never be at the mercy of things that matter least. (Goethe)
- Courage is not the absence of fear but rather the judgment that something is more important than fear. The brave may not live forever. But the cautious do not live at all. (Meg Cabot)
- So long as you open your heart to beauty, hope, cheer, courage and power, so long are you young. (Samuel Ulman). I know of no more encouraging fact than the unquestionable ability of man to elevate his life by conscious endeavor (Henry David Thoreau).

- We should encourage each other to follow the rules of considerate conduct such as think before we act, listen more, argue less, seek first to understand, think twice before asking favors, avoid shifting responsibility and blame, avoid jumping to conclusions, respect other's opinion, and enjoying the journey with your loved ones.
- If you want to achieve what you've never achieved before, you have to grow to become what you've never become before. (Brian Tracy). Insanity is doing the same over and over again and expecting different results. No problem can be solved at the same level of consciousness that created it. (Albert Einstein)
- Success and cheerfulness in life are not the result of what we have but rather how we live. What we do with the things we already have now makes the biggest difference in the quality of our life. (Tony Robbins)
- Studies have shown that companies hire for attitude and train for skills. (Singapore Airlines).
- Humility is the beginning of wisdom. (Zen habits)
- A foolish definition of success is the attainment of a certain amount of money, power, and privilege. A wise definition of success is enjoying the journey of lifelong learning with your loved ones.
- All men are created equal, endowed with the unalienable rights to life, liberty and the pursuit of happiness. (US Declaration of Independence)
- The world will be safer and prosperous when all nations adhere to the principles of peaceful coexistence where there is mutual respect for each other's territorial sovereignty and the right to self-determination and non-interference. (China-India)

- Whether a cat is black or white makes no difference. A cat that catches mice is a good cat. Whether we label an ideology socialism, capitalism, communism, or authoritarianism makes no difference. A government that can provide affordable subsidized public housing, meaningful jobs, efficient transport system, clean environment, fantastic schools, universal health care, recreation centers, and national security is a good government and should be given a strong mandate to govern. (Deng Xiaoping)

- Every nation must strive to avoid contracting the national disease of schizophrenia where there are two equally dominant sectarian political parties, bickering with each other like two juveniles. It is best if there is a political party that promote universal values that protect the rights of minorities so as to gain at least 70% of popular vote thus attaining a strong mandate to govern.

- Workers must enjoy democracy at the workplace where they have a say in the management of the company and reserve the right to buy the company if the owners decide to sell.

- All citizens must have a fair share in the prosperity of the nation. This can be achieved by practicing universal basic income (UBI) calculated as a small percentage of the living wage. UBI is able to soften the ills of neoliberalism by reducing the pain and frustration of the underprivileged who are the victims of the wealth gap between the rich and the poor. UBI is able to reduce the risk of violent civil unrest.

- Every citizen must be given universal healthcare.

- Every person has the right to demand privacy, especially when he or she has not committed any crime. (Edward Snowden)

- Every person has the right to choose his own way of life without being judged or criticized so long as he or she respects the rule of law. He can choose voluntary simplicity, country living, living off the grid, any profession, urban competition, climbing the corporate ladder, activism, the military, or politics.

- Whistleblowers should be protected by law when they expose the wrongdoings within the company or government.

Chapter seven

RELIGIOUS FRAUD

Religious fraud is a term used for civil or criminal fraud carried out in the name of a religion or within a religion. For example, a person is guilty of religious fraud when it claims that a particular food product is kosher but is found not to be kosher.

A special form of religious fraud is known as pious fraud whereby one employs lies and/or deception in order to convince others of the truth of one's own religion or specific religious claims.

A religious fraud may rely on the untenable belief that the end justify the means. The end may be the acceptance of a certain belief, but the means is not truthful. An example of a pious fraud is the Shroud of Turin which is a Medieval fabrication that supposedly was the clothing in which Jesus would have been buried.

Prosperity gospel

Of all the ways scammers can steal your money, experts agree that the most difficult fraud to combat are the ones that turn your own faith against you. Such frauds are called affinity frauds, and they happen most frequently in places of religious worship.

Ponzi schemes flourish in religion. Many religious leaders preach faith but their secret agenda is to accumulate wealth and power. Affinity fraud losses run into billions of dollars every year.

People who want to trust become vulnerable to greedy people who want to cheat. People in affinity situations such as a church or ethnic community tend to feel comfortable and let their guard down. That's when they are most open to friendly suggestions.

For example, Ephren Taylor fleeced more than $16 million from members of church flocks in 43 states in the United States by preaching prosperity gospel. "God wants you to be rich," is the resounding message, and many people fell for it.

Taylor sweet-talked many pastors into inviting him to preach to their congregations. Taylor donated generously to churches and sold promissory notes that he claimed were backed by socially responsible ventures like small businesses and affordable housing projects. But it was a Ponzi scheme.

Ephren Taylor was found guilty of religious fraud and is now serving a 19-year federal prison sentence.

Affinity fraud

In spite of a widespread crackdown on religious fraud, religious Ponzi schemes continue to flourish.

For example, Bernard Madoff focused on Jewish communities in New York and Florida. Madoff swindled more than $20 billion from the faithful.

The FBI is also investigating an affinity fraud in Utah worth around $2 billion., where 60% of the population belongs to the

Mormon Church. The church itself warned members about this affinity fraud, but they still fell for it.

Affinity scams are almost irresistible because the target audience are people who are drawn to religion through faith. So faith is the magic keyword that permit trust to take place naturally. So if you can accept sometimes with little doubt about religious myths, then you are particularly receptive to a great story line regarding investing by faith.

If the pitch on investing takes place in a religious building, your willingness to trust a religion is transferable to a willingness to trust the investment salesman. Scammers are cunning wolves in sheep clothing, targeting the weakest sheep to pounce on.

Battling false prophets

Churches must bear some responsibility when such scams happen. When churches accept this responsibility, then church leaders must not have a secret agenda to enrich themselves to allow such conflict of interest into their mindset.

Churches who are truly upright should quickly issue a written policy that states clearly as follows:

"This church will not allow any type of investment advisors or sponsors to speak from our pulpit or make presentations to our flock in the church premises or in its cell groups."

In 2016, the attorney general of Utah launched a ***White Collar Crime Offender Registry***. It is a database where anyone can enter a person's name and check whether an salesman or advisor is on that list.

But the weakness of this program is that it does not have records of scammers who cheat for the first time or has not been caught. So this scheme is only the second best strategy.

The best strategy to protect yourself from religious fraud is to become knowledgeable and doing your own independent research on investment. Find out which brokerage firms have been in the market for more than ten years. Most countries have an authority where you can make inquiries by email or make online checks. Large brokerage firms will always be on some registry with the stock exchanges, carrying the profiles of individual broker dealers.

So if your prospective advisor or their firm do not show up in official registries, this could be a red flag for you.

Religious addiction

In his book, ***When God Becomes A Drug,*** Father Leo Booth defines religious addiction as using God, a church or belief system as an escape from reality, in an attempt to find or elevate a sense of self-worth or well-being.

Symptoms include the following:

- Refusal to doubt or question authority
- Judgmental attitude
- Eating disorders
- Using fear, shame, or guilt to control others
- Eventual isolation

Booth explores the background of religious addiction, comparing the addict's progress with the stages of alcoholism and citing case histories that demonstrate the consequences of religious addiction on family members, especially children.

Father Booth recommends counseling. He outlines a self-help program for developing a healthy spirituality, using affirmation and exercises based on a rewritten version of the 12 steps of Alcoholics Anonymous. Appendixes give guidelines for intervention and professional treatment.

Spiritual but not affiliated

In his book, ***Finding Your Religion:*** *when the faith you grew up in has lost its meaning,* Scotty McLennan offers ways for the perplexed to continue their spiritual lives.

Rev Scotty is a Unitarian minister and the chaplain at Tufts University. McLennan explains that our spiritual path goes through ascending stages, namely, magic, reality, dependence, interdependence, and unity.

Spiritual but not affiliated (SBNA) also known as Spiritual but no religious (SBNR) is a popular phrase used to self-identify a life stance of spirituality that takes issue with organized religion as the sole or most valuable means of furthering spiritual growth.

Historically, the words religious and spiritual have been used synonymously to describe all the various aspects of religion. But now, spirituality can mean the pursuit of growth of one's mind, body, and soul.

Spirituality need not be related to any of the world religions because spirituality claims the unalienable rights of an individual to choose his own path of growth whereas religion refers to an organization with a bureaucracy, rules and regulations.

SBNR and SBNA are not new phenomena. They have pervaded all of history.

Is it possible to be spiritual but not religious?

Of course, you can!

You can be spiritual outside of organized religion. Hillel, the great sage from the 1st century already gives you moral support.

Even within the Christian Bible, there several minor divergence in approach to religious matter. There are the symbolic ancient history, major prophets, minor prophets, poems, different accounts about Jesus, the organizational approach of Apostle Paul, the spirituality books by James and other disciples of Jesus, and the speculative book of Revelation to frighten people.

James 1:27 NIV reads as follows:

Religion that God our Father accepts as pure and faultless is this: to look after orphans and widows in their distress and to keep oneself from being polluted by the world.

In year 2020, there are many more people in distress that require our help. If we want to be spiritual but not religious or affiliated, James's exhortation can be expanded as follows:

True religion is protecting the powerless - orphans, widows, homeless, migrant workers, disabled, and injured soldiers returning from an unnecessary war.

This can be further expanded by how we need to give power to our good intention by quoting Martin Luther King Jr:

Power without love is reckless and abusive. Love without power is sentimental and anemic. Power at its best is love implementing the demands of justice. Justice at its best is power correcting everything that stands against love.

The wisdom of Hillel

If you take a Holy Land Tour, you may begin by first arriving at Ben Gurion Airport, Tel Aviv, Israel. This airport handles around 25 million passengers in 2019. Security is high at Ben Gurion Airport because it has been the target of several terrorist attacks and hijacking of planes.

Israel has an integrated nationwide public transport system

covering multiple transit options using train, bus and light rail., and using a single payment smart card. Car rental at the airport is available from Avis, Budget, Eldan, Thrifty, Hertz, and Shlomo Sixt.

There are many tours available to see Israel itself or Jordan, Lebanon, Egypt, and so forth. A 9-day Israel Christian Heritage Tour will bring you to experience biblical sites and ancient Christian landmarks. You can relive the stories of the Bible and walk in the footsteps of Jesus of Nazareth.

You'll visit Jesus' birthplace in Bethlehem, his hometown of Nazareth, and follow the footsteps of Jesus as you walk through the Old City of Jerusalem along Dia Dolorosa towards the Church of the Holy Sepulchre.

Less well-known than Jesus of Nazareth was a great teacher of Judaism, named Hillel. But Hillel had a great message for the world, untainted by organized religion.

Who is Hillel?

According to tradition, Hillel was born around 110 BCE in Babylon. Hillel died in Jerusalem in 10 CE. Hillel was a Jewish religious teacher. Hillel was one of the most important figures in Jewish history. He is associated with the development of the Misnah and the Talmud.

Hillel was renowned within Judaism as a sage and a scholar. Hillel founded the House of Hillel School of Tannaim (Sages of the Mishnah) and the founder of a dynasty of Sages who dominated the theology of the Jews living in Israel until the fifth century.

Hillel is popularly known as the author of two famous saying:

- *If I am not for myself who is for me? And being for my own self, what am I? And if not now, when?*
- *That which is hateful to you, do not do to your fellow men.*

In a famous story from the Talmud, a pagan approached the great Rabbi Hillel and promised that he would convert to Judaism if Hillel could teach him the entire Torah standing on one leg.

Hillel replied:

What is hateful to yourself, do not do to your fellow man. That is the whole Torah and the remainder is but commentary. Go and study it.

Hillel insisted that any interpretation of scriptures that bred hatred or disdain for others - whatever their beliefs - is illegitimate.

Wisdom of principles, values & virtues

Is it possible to climb the spiritual mountain without organized religion?

My answer is YES!

Instead of looking at these spiritual stages of human development as a personal history, why not view it as the evolution of man as a species.

As we understand, your life and my life will be impacted by what's going in the 21st century war between China and the United States. The internal squabbles in the US and the protests in Hong Kong and Taiwan put pressure on national leaders to RETHINK about their policies and systems of governance.

Everyone, but especially the leaders in government, business, science and the humanities should carry out creative destruction - dumping ideas that are obsolete and no longer working, and embracing new approaches and new ideas.

Ultimately, they all boil down to principles, values, and virtues:

- **PRINCIPLES** - an accepted or professed rule of action or conduct; e.g. meritocracy, pragmatism, integrity, community and family over self
- **VALUES** - that property of a thing because of which it is esteemed, desirable, or useful or what matters most; e.g. character, purpose, freedom to vote, health, healthy relationship, empathy, faith, hope, and charity.
- **VIRTUES** - moral excellence or goodness; e.g. appreciation, moderation, frugality, chastity, humility, diligence, and understanding as opposed to the 7 deadly sins of envy, gluttony, greed, lust, pride, sloth, and wrath.

Regardless of whether you are religious or not, you have to deal with realities of your vote, health, wealth, relationships, and life purpose. There are 193 sovereign states of the United Nations out there with thousands of cultures, races, languages, and religions.

What is the common ground where we can meet others part way?

The only common ground revolves around PRINCPLES, VALUES, VIRTUES.

If this is true, then thinkers who discuss issues in terms of principles, values, and virtues would be of utmost value to all of us.

For instance, character development using ***The 7 Habits of Highly Effective People*** by Stephen Covey would be most helpful:

- **Be proactive** - don't react. Think before you act. Take time to enjoy your freedom to choose your options.
- **Begin with the end in mind** - make your nation and family great again.
- **Put first things first** - know your priority, ignore dogma, pro-

duce positive result.

- **Think win-win** - seek mutual benefits.
- **Seek first to understand, then to be understood** - listen more and seek mutual understanding, develop empathy.
- **Synergize** - the highest activity of life is creative cooperation, to join forces to do good.
- **Sharpen the saw** - to preserve and enhance the greatest asset you have - you with your body, mind, emotions, and spirit.

The new psychology of love, traditional values and spiritual growth using ***The Road Less Traveled*** by Scott Peck would be most useful.

Life is difficult. It is difficult because life is a never-ending series of problems. Taken in a proactive light, problems force us to find solution and in the process of solving our problems we grow - and we can enjoy the journey.

Love will make us willing to apply the four tools of discipline to solve all our problems:

- **Delaying of gratification** - meeting the pain first rather than the pleasure, developing patience and persistence.
- **Acceptance of responsibility** - control your destiny or someone else will.
- **Dedication to truth** - seek truth from facts, face reality as it is, not as it was or as you wish it were.
- **Balancing** - gathering information, weighing all the possibilities and wisely balancing them.

Study-activity group

What should I do if I really miss organized religion, especially the organization, beautiful music, and educational facilities?

You can form a study group with a strict code of selecting members. You start by having a few principle-centered permanent members. There must be an understanding that guests can attend your study group by invitation only.

If you feel that forming a study group may be too burdensome, make it a activity group. But you are warned that no permanent member can invite any guest without an unanimous approval from all the permanent members. The group reserves the right to refuse the attendance of any guest so as to preserve the special culture and atmosphere of this group.

A few close friends who are committed to spend a lot of time together will gather and discuss whether they want to form a study or an activity group. Use the **Six Thinking Hats** method to come to some conclusion.

An alternative way to get started is to piggyback on some organization that is already doing a great job at the community, national, or international level. If you choose to do that, then your study or activity group need not have any structure at all, since you are joining forces with an established organization.

Here are the 10 most popular NGOs where you may like to get involved with:

- **BRAC** is a Bangladeshi non-governmental development organization that was formed in 1972 by Fazle Hasan Abed. It offers its services to 64 districts in Bangladesh as well as other places in Asia, Americas and Africa. Its main services include village development programs, cooperative agriculture, rural crafts, fisheries, health and family planning, literacy, and vocational training for women, and construction of community centers.
- **Wikimedia Foundation** was founded on June 20, 2003 by Jimmy Wales. It's headquarter is in San Francisco, California,

USA. It maintains and develop open content provided to the public free of charge. It has its own political advocacy.

- **Acumen Fund** is founded by Jacqueline Novogaratz. Its headquarter is in New York City, USA. It uses its funds to solve the problems of poverty. It delivers goods and services to the poorest people and improve their lives in Kenya, India, Pakistan, and Ghana. It has created more than 60,000 jobs, and help 100 million people around the world.

- **Danish Refugee Council** is founded in 1956 as an umbrella organization for 33 member organizations. It provides services to needy and poorest people around the world, working with more than 30 countries. More than 500,000 refugees have received emergency relief such as clothes, mattresses, hygiene kits, shelters, and blankets.

- **Partners in Health** is founded by Paul Farmer, Jim Yong Kim, Ophelia Dahl Thomas J White and Todd McCormack. Its headquarter is in Boston, Massachusetts, USA. It provides medical services to the poorest areas in developing countries. It strives to remove barriers to maintain good and secure health such as the lack of clean water and food, and strengthening the rights of the poor.

- **Ceres** is founded in 1989 by Joan Bavaria. It is based in Boston, Massachusetts, USA. Its aim is to mobilize business leadership and investors to build a sustainable and thriving global economy. It brings together companies, investors, stakeholders, and public interest groups to expand and adopt sustainable business practices and solutions to build a healthy global economy.

- **CARE** stands for Cooperative for Assistance and Relief Everywhere. It was founded in 1945 by Wallace Justin Campbell and Arthur C Ringland. It delivers long term international development projects and emergency relief. It is supporting 880 poverty fighting projects in over 90 countries. It also works in the fields of climate change, water, sanitation, agriculture, emergency response, health, education, agriculture and food security.

- **Medecins Sans Frontierres** was founded in 1971 by a group of doctors. They are known as *Doctors Without Borders*. They respond to endemic diseases and launching projects in war-torn regions. It provides medical services in over 70 countries with the help of volunteer nurses, doctors, logistic experts, sanitation and water engineers, administrators, and other medical professionals.
- **Cure violence** was founded by the University of Illinois at Chicago School of Public Health Epidemiologist Gary Slutkin in 2000. Its main focus is to stop the spread of violence in communities and treating high-risk individuals and changing social norms.
- **Mercy Corps** was founded in 1979 under the name of *The Refugee Fund.* Its aim is to help in places where there are political upheavals, economic collapse, disasters, conflicts, and times of crises. Thus it works in many countries like Iraq, Afghanistan, Libya, Kenya, India, Morocco, Nepal, Pakistan, Nigeria, Jordan, Lebanon, Indonesia, Haiti, Colombia, China, DR Congo, Syria, Yemen,

Act now on your beliefs

Religious organizations must bear some responsibility when financial scams happen. When they accept this responsibility, then religious leaders must not have a secret agenda to enrich themselves to allow such conflict of interest into their mindset.

Religious organizations who are truly upright should issue a written policy that states clearly that "this religious organization will not allow any type of investment advisors or sponsors to speak from our pulpit or make presentations to our flock in our premises or in its cell groups."

We can be religious and spiritual without being affiliated to any organized religion. In this way, our conscience is clear. True religion is to protect the powerless starting with offering help to orphans and widows.

You can form a study-activity group to further your common interests and enhance your group wisdom. But be very selective in who you invite. Make principles, values, and virtues as the constitution of your study-activity group, reserving the right to refuse any troublesome guest from attending.

Always remember what true religion is:

True religion is protecting the powerless - orphans, widows, homeless, migrant workers, disabled, and injured soldiers returning from an unnecessary war.

Decisions have the power to steer and change your life forever. Therefore, nothing affects the quality of your life than your ability to make the right decisions. All that you have achieved or failed to achieved can be traced back to the decisions you've made - on issues concerning your vote, health, wealth, relationships, and life purpose.

Change your beliefs, and you will change your principles, values, virtues, habits, attitudes, social skills, ethics, behavior and so forth.

In life there are no mistakes, only lessons. The secret to resilience, happiness and a less stressful success is to avoid focusing on stagnant traits. Instead, focus on adopting an active, growth-oriented and problem-solving approach to life, and enjoying the journey together with your loved ones.

Here are the beliefs of greatness that will empower you to enjoy the journey with your loved ones:

- That which is hateful to you, do not do to your fellow human beings. Any interpretation of scriptures that bred hatred or disdain for others - whatever their beliefs - was illegitimate. (Hillel)
- True religion is protecting the powerless - orphans, widows, homeless, migrant workers, disabled, and injured soldiers returning from an unnecessary war.
- Power without love is reckless and abusive. Love without power is sentimental and anemic. Power at its best is love implementing the demands of justice. Justice at its best is power correcting everything that stands against love. (Martin Luther King)
- That which matter most must never be at the mercy of things that matter least. (Goethe)
- Courage is not the absence of fear but rather the judgment that something is more important than fear. The brave may not live forever. But the cautious do not live at all. (Meg Cabot)
- So long as you open your heart to beauty, hope, cheer, courage and power, so long are you young. (Samuel Ulman). I know of no more encouraging fact than the unquestionable ability of man to elevate his life by conscious endeavor (Henry David Thoreau).
- We should encourage each other to follow the rules of considerate conduct such as think before we act, listen more, argue less, seek first to understand, think twice before asking favors, avoid shifting responsibility and blame, avoid jump-

ing to conclusions, respect other's opinion, and enjoying the journey with your loved ones.

- If you want to achieve what you've never achieved before, you have to grow to become what you've never become before. (Brian Tracy). Insanity is doing the same over and over again and expecting different results. No problem can be solved at the same level of consciousness that created it. (Albert Einstein)
- Success and cheerfulness in life are not the result of what we have but rather how we live. What we do with the things we already have now makes the biggest difference in the quality of our life. (Tony Robbins)
- Studies have shown that companies hire for attitude and train for skills. (Singapore Airlines).
- Humility is the beginning of wisdom. (Zen habits)
- A foolish definition of success is the attainment of a certain amount of money, power, and privilege. A wise definition of success is enjoying the journey of lifelong learning with your loved ones.
- All men are created equal, endowed with the unalienable rights to life, liberty and the pursuit of happiness. (US Declaration of Independence)
- The world will be safer and prosperous when all nations adhere to the principles of peaceful coexistence where there is mutual respect for each other's territorial sovereignty and the right to self-determination and non-interference. (China-India)
- Whether a cat is black or white makes no difference. A cat that catches mice is a good cat. Whether we label an ideology socialism, capitalism, communism, or authoritarianism makes no difference. A government that can

provide affordable subsidized public housing, meaningful jobs, efficient transport system, clean environment, fantastic schools, universal health care, recreation centers, and national security is a good government and should be given a strong mandate to govern. (Deng Xiaoping)

- Every nation must strive to avoid contracting the national disease of schizophrenia where there are two equally dominant sectarian political parties, bickering with each other like two juveniles. It is best if there is a political party that promote universal values that protect the rights of minorities so as to gain at least 70% of popular vote thus attaining a strong mandate to govern.

- Workers must enjoy democracy at the workplace where they have a say in the management of the company and reserve the right to buy the company if the owners decide to sell.

- All citizens must have a fair share in the prosperity of the nation. This can be achieved by practicing universal basic income (UBI) calculated as a small percentage of the living wage. UBI is able to soften the ills of neoliberalism by reducing the pain and frustration of the underprivileged who are the victims of the wealth gap between the rich and the poor. UBI is able to reduce the risk of violent civil unrest.

- Every citizen must be given universal healthcare.

- Every person has the right to demand privacy, especially when he or she has not committed any crime. (Edward Snowden)

- Every person has the right to choose his own way of life without being judged or criticized so long as he or she respects the rule of law. He can choose voluntary simplicity, country living, living off the grid, any profession, urban competition, climbing the corporate ladder, activism, the military, or politics.

- Whistleblowers should be protected by law when they expose the wrongdoings within the company or government.

Chapter eight

FAKE SCIENCE

In the 1980s, the drug companies struck on an brilliant idea - Why not make more money just like we did for the health care industry by labeling patients with emotional problems as mentally ill, and pushing prescription of brain drugs for patients?

Just like the emergence of religion, psychiatry began to move towards the dark side.

The vast majority of psychiatrists who used to counsel patients on positive mental attitude and making better life decisions now gather together to list symptoms such as depression, anxiety, and compulsions as mental illnesses that can be treated using brain drugs. Drugs companies branded their drugs with impressive names such as Prozac, Zoloft, Paxil, Ritalin and so forth.

Many of the brain drugs will do permanent damage to your nervous system when taken long term.

Hazardous science

In his book, ***Warning: psychiatry can be hazardous to your mental health,*** Dr. William Glasser, reveals the hazards that psychiatry can present to you:

- You may be diagnosed as mentally ill when you are not.
- You may be given brain drugs to treat your non-existent illness.
- These brain drugs have side effects that are similar to symptoms of Parkinson's disease.

You may be declared insane thus robbing you of your rights. On the flip side, people feign insanity to obtain financial compensation, housing, drugs, avoid work, military duty or criminal prosecution. This is called malingering.

One hilarious case involved Vincent Gigante. They called him the "Oddfather." He was boss of New York's Genovese Mafia. To avoid jail time, Gigante feigned insanity. He would wander around Greenwich village with a bathrobe and slippers. He would stop abruptly, point at things and start mumbling gibberish.

If he thought for sure that he was being taped or filmed by the feds, Gigante would really lay it thick. He would ask parking meters if they would join him on a walk. Once, FBI agents arrived with a subpoena only to find him standing naked in a running shower clutching an open umbrella.

Official records from many countries report massive fraud in the mental health care industry. Financial fraud amounts to billions of dollars paid out by governments and health insurance companies each year. Psychiatrists and psychologists have practically zero accountability.

Citizen Commission on Human Rights International regularly present information as a public service to law enforcement agencies, health care fraud investigators, international police agencies, medical and psychological licensing boards and the general public.

Gun violence

Random gun violence is a terrifying fact of American life. This is because of both the violence and the randomness. It is the randomness that breeds terror.

The explanation for this is that such killers involved have mental illness. This sounds reasonable enough for the general public. But epidemiologic research says otherwise. Only 4% of these violent criminals have mental problems. Most violent behavior are due to factors other than mental illness.

The actual risk factors are growing up as a spoiled child, taking drugs, drinking alcohol, depression, unhappiness, taking revenge, racism, inferiority complex, superiority complex, making wrong assumptions, lack of training and oversight.

This say story will demonstrate several risk factors.

In Chapter 6 of his book, ***BLINK, the power of thinking without thinking,*** Malcolm Gladwell relates a case of making three thinking mistakes in seven seconds in the Bronx.

The 110 block of Wheeler Avenue in South Bronx was a very old building in a poor and working class neighborhood. Amadou Diallo, a 22-year-old from Guinea, lived there. He peddled videotapes, socks and gloves at lower Manhattan. Diallo was short and unassuming.

On the night of February 19, 1999, Diallo returned to his apartment in the second floor close to midnight. He went downstairs and stood at the top of the steps of his apartment building to relax.

A few minutes later, four white plainclothes police officers in an unmarked Ford Taurus. turned slowly into Wheeler Avenue. They wore bulletproof vests and all four carried police-issue 9-

mm semi-automatic handguns.

When the police officers spotted Dallio, they jumped to the wrong assumption that Dallio might be the look-out for robbers. They also thought, wrongly, that Dallio fitted the description of a serial rapist.

One of the officers shouted, "Police. Can we have a word?"

Dallio had a stutter. His English was bad, and he was terrified that these men might be the robbers that robbed someone he knew. So Dallio tried to ran into the apartment building but the door couldn't open quickly enough. Dallio reached into his pocket to try and retrieve some black object. One of the officers shouted, "Gun! He's got a gun," and they opened fire."

Fake science

David Rosenhan, professor of psychology at Stanford University conducted an experiment to determine the validity of psychiatric diagnosis. Participants in this experiment feigned hallucinations at several psychiatric hospitals and were duly admitted.

These pseudo-patients were diagnosed with all forms of psychiatric disorders and were given anti-psychiatric drugs. When these pseudo-patients told the hospital staff that they no longer experience hallucinations, they were ignored and had to stay on the average of two weeks in hospital.

An offended psychiatric hospital administration, upon discovering that this was a university experiment, challenged Dr. Rosenhan to send pseudo-patients to its facility and it could easily identify them as pseudo-patients. Rosenhan agreed.

After several weeks, this psychiatric hospital reported to Rosenhan that out of the 250 new patients admitted, its staff could identify 41 of them. Rosenhan informed the hospital that he did not send any pseudo-patient to the hospital.

Dr Robert L Spitzer is considered by some to be the father of modern psychiatry. In 2003, Dr.Spitzer did a poorly conceived investigation to conclude that homosexuality is a mental illness that can be cured by using brain drugs.

Nine years later, Dr. Spitzer suffered from Parkinson's disease. He had trouble walking, sitting or keeping his head up. But he staggered slowly to his computer, to type out his apology for backing the "cure" for homosexuality.

Suicide

The World Health Organization (WHO) estimates that each year, about one million people die from suicide. This represents a global mortality rate of 16 people per 100,000 or one death every 40 seconds. Suicide rates around the world are rising steadily over the years.

Suicide is the next step from prolonged depression. Suicides, depression and stress result from many complex sociocultural and economic factors several of them being as follow:

- Loss of a loved one.
- Persistent unemployment or great financial loss.
- Sexual orientation.
- Difficulties in developing one's identity.
- Disassociation from one's family, community or other social/ belief group.
- Disability related to disease, old age, and extreme sleep deprivation.
- Job burnout - a state of physical, emotional, and mental

exhaustion combined with doubts about your competence, the value of your work, and loss of meaning.

- Honor - willing to sacrifice one's life for a cause or to remain true to one's values.
- Public disapproval, criticism, physical and cyber bullying
- Police harassment and torture

Dealing with depression naturally

In 1980, researchers at Texas University Medical Center decided to take a medical approach to helping psychiatric patients. Some 100 psychiatric patients were given a complete medical examination comprising historical records, physical examination, and lab tests.

They discovered that 80% of them had some physical illness, such as hyperthyroidism, hypothyroidism, nutritional deficiencies, cancer, diabetes, chronic fatigue syndrome, viral infection, infectious hepatitis, multiple sclerosis, candida syndrome, hypoglycemia, brain allergies and so forth.

These patients showed significant signs of recovery when they were given appropriate supplements such as tryptophan, S-adenosylmethione (SAM), 5-HTP, tyrosine, phenyllalanine, gamma aminobutyric acid (GABA), choline, lecithin, inositol, carnitine, kelp, linseed oil, fish oil, gamm-linolenic acid, riboflavin, selenium, DHEA (dehydroepiandrosterone), vitamins A, B, C, D, K, calcium, lithium, magnesium, zinc, iron, copper, St. John's wort, black cohosh, damiana, ginkgo biloba, ginseng, gotu kola, lemon balm, valerian, vitex agnus-castus L, and yohimbe.

Do your own independent research and review. Be vigilant. Get your supplements from the most established suppliers. Never overdose. You should underdose, especially if you are taking many supplements. Some of these supplements may not do well for you.

Additionally, patients were also found to have a high level of heavy metal poisoning by lead, aluminum, copper, mercury, formaldehyde, pesticides, and plastics.

Foods that will detox the body and lighten your liver's work load are as follow:

Coriander, parsley, broccoli, kale, proteins from eggs and fish, chlorella, alpha lipoic acid found in spinach, broccoli, peas, Brussel sprouts, rice, bran and organic meats, and pectin found in the rinds of green apples, cabbage, banana, beets, grapes, carrots, and pith from citrus fruits.

Prevention of depression

One ounce of prevention is far better than one ton of cure.

Just like thinking, swimming, and any other skill, mental toughness can be improved.

This is a belief.

Do you accept the validity of this statement?

Even though we talk about mental toughness, it involves all your four dimensions - namely, physical, mental, socio-emotional, and spiritual. The root of depression is the feeling of powerlessness. But when you think of solving all problems in terms of MEANING & RESPONSIBILITY, your inner spiritual stamina will grow.

In his book, ***The Road Less Traveled****: a new psychology pf love, traditional values and spiritual growth*, Scott Peck, a psychiatrist, explains that life is difficult. When we we truly see this truth, once we truly know that life is difficult, we transcend it. Life then is no longer difficult. Because once this truth is accepted, the fact that life is difficult no longer matters.

It's a matter of adopting a good healthy attitude. It is not wise to be stubborn and fixed in your ideas.

Life is a series of problems Discipline is the basic set of tools we require to solve them. Without discipline we can solve nothing. We some discipline we solve some problems. With full discipline we solve all problems.

There are four tools of discipline:

- **Delaying of gratification** (facing the pain first ahead of the pleasure - homework before TV, impulse control, patience, persistence)
- **Acceptance of responsibility** ("This is my problem, and I am responsible to solve it.")
- **Dedication to truth** (face reality as it is, not as it was, or as you wish it were)
- **Balancing** (there are many factors to consider; you must put first thing first and last thing last; you may need to accept trade-offs, be flexible , innovative...)

As you can see, these are not complex tools that require extensive training. These are simple tools that almost all children are adept in their use by the age of ten.

So the problem lies not in the complexity of these tools but the willingness to use them. This willingness to use these four tools of discipline is LOVE.

Dr. Peck defines LOVE as the WILL to extend one's self for the purpose of nurturing one's own or another's spiritual growth.

There are many ways to strengthen our mental toughness:

- Competitive sports

- Outward Bound School
- Scout & girl guide movement
- Basic martial arts training
- Camping and living off the grid for a while
- Self-knowledge, using psychometric tests
- Professional training - have marketable skills
- Financial and investment education
- Public speaking and conversational skills
- Emotional intelligence sessions
- Spiritual journey by reading up to 500 pages of information a day

Lighten your emotional load

The basis to lighten your emotional load is to establish a wise definition of success.

A foolish definition of success is to attain a certain quantity of money, power and privilege. This materialistic approach to life will lead to a tragic ending.

A wise definition of success is more like this - Success is enjoying the journey with your loved ones.

Focus on this one wise definition of success, and you'll have a happy ending.

It is better to dig just one well 100 feet deep than 10 wells 10 feet deep. Say NO to almost everything else. Stay focus on this wonderful objective - to enjoy the journey every day with your loved ones.

If your attitude stinks and it is affecting your relationship with your loved ones - transform your attitude.

You'll achieve more resilience, success, and joy - with just one thought - GROW SPIRITUALLY. Listen more and talk less. Don't argue. Use the ***Six Thinking Hats*** to consider all aspects of an issue. Be more understanding, be more flexible, be less judgmental and you'll do just fine. Emotional intelligence is far more important than IQ or looks. Focus on growth, not traits.

Start internalizing these beliefs of greatness and you'll make your nation and your family great again!

Act now on your beliefs

Recognize that psychiatry is healthy if it is a way of counseling patients. But when a psychiatrist is pushing brain drugs, he is your enemy because brain drugs may permanently damage your nervous system.

When you suffer clinical depression, take the first step of healing your body. Getting a complete medical examination should be your first response. Then take the appropriate supplements and foods. Exercise regularly, have quality sleep, develop your social intelligence, master your investing skills and you will achieve peak performance and personal renewal.

Decisions have the power to steer and change your life forever. Therefore, nothing affects the quality of your life than your ability to make the right decisions. All that you have achieved or failed to achieved can be traced back to the decisions you've made - on issues concerning your vote, health, wealth, relationships, and life purpose.

Change your beliefs, and you will change your principles, values, virtues, habits, attitudes, social skills, ethics, behavior and so forth.

In life there are no mistakes, only lessons. The secret to resilience, happiness and a less stressful success is to avoid focusing on stagnant traits. Instead, focus on adopting an active, growth-oriented and problem-solving approach to life, and enjoying the journey together with your loved ones.

Here are the beliefs of greatness that will empower you to enjoy the journey with your loved ones:

- That which is hateful to you, do not do to your fellow human beings. Any interpretation of scriptures that bred hatred or disdain for others - whatever their beliefs - is illegitimate. (Hillel)
- True religion is protecting the powerless - orphans, widows, homeless, migrant workers, disabled, and injured soldiers returning from an unnecessary war.
- Power without love is reckless and abusive. Love without power is sentimental and anemic. Power at its best is love implementing the demands of justice. Justice at its best is power correcting everything that stands against love. (Martin Luther King)
- That which matter most must never be at the mercy of things that matter least. (Goethe)
- Courage is not the absence of fear but rather the judgment that something is more important than fear. The brave may not live forever. But the cautious do not live at all. (Meg Cabot)
- So long as you open your heart to beauty, hope, cheer, courage and power, so long are you young. (Samuel Ulman). I know of no more encouraging fact than the unquestionable ability of man to elevate his life by conscious endeavor (Henry David Thoreau).
- We should encourage each other to follow the rules of con-

siderate conduct such as think before we act, listen more, argue less, seek first to understand, think twice before asking favors, avoid shifting responsibility and blame, avoid jumping to conclusions, respect other's opinion, and enjoying the journey with your loved ones.

- If you want to achieve what you've never achieved before, you have to grow to become what you've never become before. (Brian Tracy). Insanity is doing the same over and over again and expecting different results. No problem can be solved at the same level of consciousness that created it. (Albert Einstein)
- Success and cheerfulness in life are not the result of what we have but rather how we live. What we do with the things we already have now makes the biggest difference in the quality of our life. (Tony Robbins)
- Studies have shown that companies hire for attitude and train for skills. (Singapore Airlines).
- Humility is the beginning of wisdom. (Zen habits)
- A foolish definition of success is the attainment of a certain amount of money, power, and privilege. A wise definition of success is enjoying the journey of lifelong learning with your loved ones.
- All men are created equal, endowed with the unalienable rights to life, liberty and the pursuit of happiness. (US Declaration of Independence)
- The world will be safer and prosperous when all nations adhere to the principles of peaceful coexistence where there is mutual respect for each other's territorial sovereignty and the right to self-determination and non-interference. (China-India)
- Whether a cat is black or white makes no differ-

ence. A cat that catches mice is a good cat. Whether we label an ideology socialism, capitalism, communism, or authoritarianism makes no difference. A government that can provide affordable subsidized public housing, meaningful jobs, efficient transport system, clean environment, fantastic schools, universal health care, recreation centers, and national security is a good government and should be given a strong mandate to govern. (Deng Xiaoping)

- Every nation must strive to avoid contracting the national disease of schizophrenia where there are two equally dominant sectarian political parties, bickering with each other like two juveniles. It is best if there is a political party that promote universal values that protect the rights of minorities so as to gain at least 70% of popular vote thus attaining a strong mandate to govern.
- Workers must enjoy democracy at the workplace where they have a say in the management of the company and reserve the right to buy the company if the owners decide to sell.
- All citizens must have a fair share in the prosperity of the nation. This can be achieved by practicing universal basic income (UBI) calculated as a small percentage of the living wage. UBI is able to soften the ills of neoliberalism by reducing the pain and frustration of the underprivileged who are the victims of the wealth gap between the rich and the poor. UBI is able to reduce the risk of violent civil unrest.
- Every citizen must be given universal healthcare.
- Every person has the right to demand privacy, especially when he or she has not committed any crime. (Edward Snowden)
- Every person has the right to choose his own way of life without being judged or criticized so long as he or she respects the rule of law. He can choose voluntary simplicity,

country living, living off the grid, any profession, urban competition, climbing the corporate ladder, activism, the military, or politics.

- Whistleblowers should be protected by law when they expose the wrongdoings within the company or government.

Chapter nine

MEDICAL FRAUD

Monsanto Company started out in 1901 manufacturing controversial products such as DDT, PCBs, and recombinant bovine growth hormone. Its seed patenting model was criticized as biopiracy and a threat to biodiversity.

Monsanto was called an evil corporation because it produced Agent Orange, a defoliant chemical, used in Vietnam War. 3 million hectares of land in Vietnam were exposed to this poison.

Up to four million people in Vietnam were exposed to Agent Orange. US veterans also suffered illnesses along with Vietnamese who were exposed to this poison. Agent Orange caused such illnesses as leukemia, Hodgkin's lymphoma, and various kinds of cancer. Monsanto said that it was the US government that bought this defoliant to use in a war.

Monsanto was headquartered in Creve Coeur, Missouri. Monsanto developed Roundup, a glyphosate-based herbicide in the 1970s. It was a major producer of genetically engineered crops which had proven to be hazardous to human beings.

Monsanto celebrated its approval of its dicamba herbicide by the US Food & Drugs Administration (FDA). However, Monsanto suffered a major financial blow when a US jury ruled that the company was liable for a terminally ill man's cancer, who was subsequently awarded $289 million.

Dewayne Johnson was a 46-year-old former groundskeeper. The jury found that Monsanto did not warn his customers of the health hazards from exposure. Johnson's lawyers argued that Monsanto fought science for years, fighting dirty to silence cancer scientists.

The presiding judge allowed lawyers to present scientific arguments in court. Monsanto had repeatedly ignored experts' warnings. Monsanto was found guilty of bribing scientists and even Scientific American magazine to publish ghostwritten articles to support the continued usage of hazardous products.

In June, 2018, Bayer of Germany acquired Monsanto for $66 billion after gaining US and EU regulatory approval.

In May 2019, a California jury ordered Bayer to pay $2 billion in damages to a Livermore couple for causing cancer with Monsanto's Roundup product.

Around 47,000 people have filed suit against Monsanto Company alleging that exposure to Roundup herbicide caused them or their loved ones to develop non-Hodgkin lymphoma, and that Monsanto covered up the risks.

As part of the discovery process, Monsanto had to turn over millions of pages of its internal records, now known as the Monsanto Papers. They provided sufficient evidence to show that Monsanto Company did perpetuate these wrongdoings.

The evils of big pharma

The pharmaceutical industry is doing more than $1 trillion of business each year. They make money on our sickness, not our health. The sicker you are, the more the health care industry profit. The healthier you are, the less money it will make.

Most of the largest pharmaceutic companies are in the US - Johnson & Johnson, Pfizer, Merck, and Eli Lilly. It spends more than $2 billion in its lobbying efforts. Together with the health insurance industry and the American Medical Association, they form the unholy alliance to monopolize medical care and charge sky-high medical fees, ten times that of Canada across the border.

We may complain about China subsidizing Chinese State-Owned Enterprises and giant public companies to outcompete most other companies. In the same vein, Big Pharma fund medical education and administration to slant business in Big Pharma's favor.

Why are they doing this?

To control what is being taught in medical school. Doctors, hospitals, and medical experts are all given incentives to boost sales of drugs, no matter how poisonous they are.

Big pharmaceutical companies use an evil business model that provide quick fixes to manage diseases, and make tons of money to keep patients coming back for more and more medication.

As early as 2003, drug company insiders are beginning to confess more openly that the vast majority of drugs work in only 30 to 50% of patients. And almost all the drugs have mild to serious side effects such as micro-bleeding, dementia, and so forth.

Doctors seldom warn you that X-rays and scans will damage your DNA. Aluminum is found in vaccines. Vaccines may also cause the very disease that they are suppose to prevent. Many annual tests do more harm than good. Many common drugs increase the risk of dementia.

Risky expensive medications

In 2011, a group of influential dermatologists issued a set of national guidelines for treating psoriasis. The recommended medication comprises a class of immunity-suppression drugs that could be used to clear up mild skin issues before weddings or other special events.

In 2012, ABBVie created a "Nurse Ambassador" program that paid nurses to go around the country to make home visits to patients who were prescribed Humira, its rheumatoid arthritis and psoriasis drug.

AbbVie specially instructed these nurses not to mention the risks of the drug which include potentially deadly infections and cancer.

California Department of Insurance filed a lawsuit claiming $1.2 billion against AbbVie alleging that AbbVie paid kickbacks to doctors to prescribe the drug and sent nurses into homes to keep patients on a dangerous drug at any cost.

In 2014, Pfizer paid 12 experts to author a comparative analysis of different medications for rheumatoid arthritis and to give the conclusion that Pfizer's Xeljanz is the most effective medication.

All of the above were part of a massive push by drugmakers to boost the sale of expensive immunity-suppressing drugs to treat autoimmune conditions such as psoriasis and rheumatoid arthritis. Patients were not warned of serious side effects.

Opioid epidemic

More Americans died of drug overdose than in the entire Vietnam War.

Investigations revealed that Mallinckrodt, a pharmaceutical company flooded Florida with hundreds of millions of oxycodone pills.

Dr. Russell Portenoy was an influential president of the American Pain Society. Portenoy traveled around the country since the 1980s showing videos touting opioids as wonder drugs, urging doctors to use them aggressively to relieve pain.

Dr. Portenoy said that the likelihood of an opioid drug as prescribed by a doctor leading to addiction is extremely low, which is not true.

One of the doctors that followed Dr. Portenoy's recommendation was Dr. Barry Schultz. But his greed began to take over. Whistleblowers came forth to report to DEA (Drug Enforcement Administration). Most states had stringent control on opioids. Florida is the most lax.

By year 2000, Schultz was doing business rather than treating patients in Florida. Doctors, drug dealers, opioid users and drug abusers were flocking to his clinic to do whole sale business. Dr. Schultz even prescribed 1,000 opioid pills to a pregnant woman.

Many lawsuits had been filed against Dr. Portenoy, Dr. Schultz and several other doctors.

Medical errors

In 2000, Dr. Barbara Starfield did a research that uncovered a shocking fact - that 225,000 Americans died of medical errors of doctors in a single year. She published her study in the Journal of the American Medical Association (JAMA) that stated that doctors are the 3rd leading cause of death in the US.

The articles showed the following statistics:

- 12,000 died from unnecessary surgery
- 7,000 died from medication errors in hospitals

- 20,000 died from other errors in hospital
- 80,000 died from hospital-related infections
- 106,000 died from the negative side effects of drugs taken as prescribed

These numbers would be very much higher when other causes of death are included - such as diagnostic errors, errors in omission, and failure to follow guidelines. When these are added, these numbers would swell to more than 440,000 deaths each year in the US, caused by errors doctors made.

Debunking cancer myths

The drug companies, doctors, nurses, and hospital are so good at promoting their services that the very mention of the word "cancer" causes people to panic. Remember the last time the medical establishment recommended vegetable oils as a healthy replacement of butter? Later research proved that butter is healthier than vegetable oils. It's more of the question of keeping the ratio of Omega 6 and Omega 3 one to one.

So let's debunk the 4 cancer myths:

Myth #1 Patients have only a few months to live
It's true that if you are in the last stage of cancer, your life will be shortened. The big question is why should you procrastinate in leading a more healthier lifestyle? Additionally, this does not mean that you have only one choice and that is to accept whatever your doctor recommend. Failure rate is very high irrespective of how much you spend. There are many natural ways of preventing and fighting cancer which has a higher rate of success and at much lower costs.

Myth #2 Early diagnosis is recommended

Doctors advise you to diagnose early and get medication. It is a great sales pitch. But it is a half-truth. It's not the question of being diagnosed early and given medication.

Your body seeks homeostasis. Medication disrupt this homeostasis - that's why side effects appear.

Your aim should be to avoid getting the first medication. One medication will add to another to form a cascade, and you're locked into taking medication for the rest of your life. One ounce of prevention is far better than one ton of cure.

The focus should not be on diagnosis but on self-examination of all aspects of your lifestyle - sleep, stress management, exercise, avoiding toxic food and environment, proper nutrition eating wholesome food, preferably organic produce, and more plant-based. Black cumin oil inhibit tumor growth.

Toxins are the primary cause of cancer and other diseases. So detoxing your body and avoiding taking carcinogenic substances found in foods, air, and water will reduce the risk of cancer. Man has created over 100,000 chemical compounds that are spewed or spilled into the soil, air, and water. You have to avoid taking them into your body

Myth #3 You must accept nausea, hair loss, and other miseries in cancer therapy

The fact is that there are natural ways that don't put you through such miseries. Diet, exercise, sleep, and stress management play important roles to help your body stay cancer-free, or if you have early stages of cancer, to reverse it. Foods that will help you stay cancer free are raw garlic, cruciferous vegetables, green tea, berries, leafy greens, cooked tomatoes, carrots, and wine (resveratol).

Myth 4 Doctors will recommend alternative treatment if they are really effective

The fact is that if you are in the US, Big Pharma has lobbied to make it is an offence to recommend any treatment other than chemotherapy, surgery and radiation. Most doctors are not trained in nutritional science. Again the solution is to lead a healthier lifestyle before you get cancer. You can eat to fight disease. There are also effective cures in other countries that do not require chemotherapy, surgery and radiation. Many doctors recommend these three evils as a business. Most doctors don't do it on themselves or their loved ones.

Debunking diabetes myths

You have already been informed every year that more than 400,000 deaths are caused by medical errors.

Your doctor will make mistakes trying to treat your diabetes. So let's debunk some of these diabetes myths:

Myth #1 Lowering your blood sugar with meds will keep you safe.

The fact is that it is safer to stay away from any medication. A major study found that patients who used medications to lower their blood sugar as doctors recommended actually suffered the highest rate of death. Avandia, the world's leading diabetes prescription medication caused 200,000 heart attacks during the first 11 years of use.

Myth #2 Type 2 diabetes cannot be reversed

Type 2 diabetes is easier to reverse than cancer. It can be reverse by adopting a healthier lifestyle - proper diet, intermittent fasting, exercise, sunshine, quality sleep, stress management, and selected supplements. Organic wholesome foods contain bioactive compounds that are as effective as medication. For example, natural alternative to Metformin are aloe vera, alpha-lipoic acid, berberine, black plum, fenugreek, gymnema, prickly pear castus, pycnogenol and vitamin D.

Myth #3 Your genes caused type 2 diabetes

Research shows that 90% of all type 2 diabetes are almost entirely caused by an unhealthy lifestyle. Genes can be switched on or off by epigenetic factors - immediate environment of your cells and mitochondria - which are affected by lifestyle factors.

Myth #4 Patients with type 2 diabetes need to monitor their blood sugar regularly

This is a big waste of time. It is better to monitor your lifestyle factors - paying attention to all the various factors of lifestyle - diet, exercise, sunshine, quality sleep, stress management and avoiding toxic foods, drinks, air, and water.

Myths about cholesterol and heart attack

Doctors tell you that statins are effective at lowering cholesterol and protecting a heart attack and stroke. But at what cost?

Statins include atorvastatin (Lipitor), fluvastatin (Lescol XL), lovastatin (Altoprev), pitavastatin (Livalo), pravastatin (Pravachol), rosuvastatin (Crestor, Ezallor) and simvastatin

(Zocor, FloLipid). You are advised not to take them. They have serious side effects.

Some of the side effects of these statins are muscle pain, muscle damage, digestive problems and mental fuzziness. Statins may raise your blood sugar level which then leads to type 2 diabetes.. In some rare cases, statins may damage your liver.

Additionally, statins may react with other medication you may be taking that will exacerbate these side effects. The safer alternative is to know what to eat to beat disease (Dr. William Li).

Cholesterol is not the cause of cardiovascular diseases. It is your unhealthy lifestyle that will lead to these diseases.

If an alien were to hover over the earth and study road accidents, what will be his conclusion taking the same approach as doctors do?

What the alien observes is that whenever there is an accident, there is at least one ambulance on site. So the alien concludes that it is the ambulance that cause the accident. Of course, at this scale, the alien will correct his conclusion. But in the human body, processes involving cholesterol and other biochemicals are more microscopic and less observable. Don't think that there is no guesswork in medical science when it comes to microscopic processes. Cholesterol does not cause heart attacks.

Conventional narrative says that heart attacks are caused by arterial plaque formation. But did you know that you have many smaller blood vessels that feed your heart?

Looking at possible arterial blockages in post-mortem autopsy studies revealed that only 18% were actually blocked. This means that in 82% of the cases, the cause of the heart attack was not a blocked artery.

There are accumulating evidences indicating that while

clogged arteries do play a part in stroke and heart attacks, one real cause of heart attack is decreased parasympathetic tone followed by sympathetic nervous system activation and/or collateral blood circulation failure. The later is easily preventable and treated.

In Germany, g-strophanthine (ouabin) has long been used to prevent and treat angina (chest pain). Enhanced external counterpulsation (EECP) is a safe and effective alternative to bypass surgery.

Studies have shown that deeper belly fat that pad your internal organs is metabolically active as a source of ill health. If your waist measures 35 or more inches for women or 40 or more inches for men, you are harboring a potentially dangerous amount of deep belly fat.

Corporations rule the world. Pharmaceutical companies - big pharma in short - rule the field of health care, the food industry, and agriculture. This situation is ten times worse in the United States than in Canada and many other countries around the world. Wholesome foods contain bio-active compounds that are just as effective as dangerous drugs prescribed by doctors but without the side effects, and they cost ten times less.

To be fair, the medical establishment cannot take the full blame. Most people are plainly not disciplined enough to adhere to the discipline of preventive health care. So when medical issues arise, the doctors and hospital are ready to provide the quick fixes - like medication, radiation, surgery, and physiotherapy.

Fatigue

Cheerfulness and high energy are the hallmarks of great health.

Depression and fatigue or low energy is the hallmark of poor health. Fatigue is a tiredness that is lingering, constant, and limiting.

Fatigue has many causes. So the first thing to do is to go through the checklist of possible causes and eliminate them one by one by healthy living:

Stress management. Chronic fatigue is caused by anxiety, depression and anxiety coming from worries, and stress coming from long working hours, work, relationship, money and health worries. You may need to make the necessary adjustments such as changing job, getting more training, counseling, exercising more, and getting quality sleep.

Sleep debt. Chronic sleep deprivation leads to diseases. So make sure you have at least 7 hours of quality sleep every night. You may need to buy a fitness tracker that gives you a sleep analysis to any deficient sleep phase. Take a sleep aid if you have to.

Anemia. Anemia is a common blood condition where you don't have enough red blood cells. Anemia may cause some dizziness, feeling cold, and irritable. This may be due to blood loss from hemorrhoids, ulcer, or cancer. You may not be producing enough red blood cells, or you may be deficient in iron.

Allergies. All diseases starts in the gut. The microbiome provides 75% of your immunity. Your fatigue may be caused by allergies and hay fever. Many allergies may be cleared by spring cleaning out your gut with pre-biotics and pro-biotics. This may require a diet with plenty of vegetables, fruits, nuts, seeds, and healthy fats. Medication should always be the last and not your first resort.

Fibromyalgia. If you have deep muscle pain and pain at the joints, you may have fibromyalgia. If this condition cannot be reduced even after you had quality sleep, you may have this condition. See whether exercise and better diet will help.

Rheumatoid arthritis. Symptoms of rheumatoid arthritis are morning stiffness, pain and swelling in the joints. Again all these symptoms will disappear when you start your healthy living.

Type 2 diabetes. Symptoms are extreme fatigue, increased thirst, always hungry, increased urination, and unusual weight loss. You can treat this condition by exercising, losing weight, and avoiding simple sugar and processed foods.

Hypothyroidism. Underactive thyroid gives out the symptoms of fatigue, depression, cold intolerance, and weight gain. Hashimoto's thyroiditis is a common autoimmune disorder when not enough thyroid hormone is produced. You may be deficient in iodine. Take sea weeds regularly.

Addison's disease. Its symptoms include fatigue, weight loss, loss of appetite, fainting due to low blood pressure, salt craving, nausea, abdominal pain, depression and body hair loss. Making healthier lifestyle choices. Natural treatment of Addison's disease uses ginger, green tea, turmeric, Reishi mushrooms, Astragus, milk thistle, and Echinacea.

Adrenal fatigue syndrome. Your body's waste management team comprises your liver, kidneys, skin, and intestines. Having optimized liver health is important. Cortisol is the body's anti-stress hormone. It is secreted by the adrenal glands. Stress can come from metabolic sources such as high intake of sugar, toxins, and saturated fats. Physical stress comes from over-exercising. Emotional stress can come from money worries, and relationship problems. Taking care of your liver will also benefit the health of your kidneys, gall bladder, and adrenal glands. If you have to, take quality supplements that contain such ingredients as Ashwagandha, vitamins, Siberian ginseng, goji, Acai, pomegranate extracts and so forth.

Constipation. Chronic fatigue may emanate from constipation. Ideally, you need to clear your bowels everyday. This is the gold standard. This is even more important when you love to eat meat. Don't let your wastes stay in your gut too long. It may cause you health problems. Eat lots of high fiber vegetables, fruits, nuts, and seeds. And remember to drink warm filtered water throughout the day, totaling at least 2 liters.

As we discussed earlier, doctors advise you to diagnose early and get medication. It is a great sales pitch. But it is a half-truth.

It's not the question of being diagnosed early and given medication. Your aim should be to avoid getting the first medication. One medication will add to another to form a cascade, and you're locked into taking medication for the rest of your life. One ounce of prevention is far better than one ton of cure. Stay healthy through healthy living to ensure that you stay away from medication.

Do you know that it takes two years to replenish your good bacteria killed by anti-biotics?

Did your good doctor tell you that?

Instead of focusing on diagnosis, you should focus on self-examination of all aspects of your lifestyle - avoiding toxic food and environment, sleep, stress management, exercise, proper nutrition eating wholesome food, preferably organic produce, and more plant-based. Black cumin oil inhibit tumor growth.

Gut health

As you see above, there are so many factors that you must take care of in order to be healthy and cheerful.

Some of you may ask:

Are all these factors equally important?

Is there one factor which may be the most important?

Great questions!

There is one factor more important than all the other factors - ***GUT HEALTH***.

The great Hippocrates is absolutely right when he said, "All diseases begin in the gut."

Researchers on blue zones were puzzled when they discovered that centenarians lead different lifestyles. Some were fat, many smoke and drink, and yet they live pass 100. Why?

Great gut health. That the common denominator.

When your gut is healthy, you'll live long and feel happy.

The gastrointestinal tract is an organ system which takes in food, digests it to extract and absorb nutrients, and expels the remaining waste as feces.

The gastrointestinal tract comprises the mouth, esophagus, stomach, small intestine, large intestine (colon), and anus. The accessory organs of digestion are the tongue, salivary glands, pancreas, gall bladder, and liver.

The absorption surface of the small intestine, represented by finger-like structures (villi and microvilli), has an area the size of a tennis court to ensure that no nutrient is wasted. The gut comprises the small and large intestines.

The brain and the gut are connected both physically and biochemically. The brain and the gut have 100 billion and 500 million neurons respectively. There are several nerves connecting the brain with the gut. The largest nerve in the gut-brain axis is the vagus nerve.

The vagus nerve carries signals in both directions to control appetite, feelings, emotions, anxiety, depression, stress, body clock, and sleep. A reduced tone in the vagus nerve will cause gastrointestinal problems such as irritable bowel syndrome and Crohn's disease.

Researchers discovered that it is your microbiome in your gut that is the key factor in determining your health and longevity. It is your main line of defense against pathogenic microbes and chemicals.

What is microbiome?

Microbiome comprises many colonies of bacteria, viruses, parasites and other microbes living in your gut.

Specific species of bacteria have specialized functions. They help in fighting inflammation, diseases, and repair your gut lining. So when you are deficient in these specific species of bacteria, you'll fall sick of a specific disease.

Microbes, gut cells, and the brain produce neurotransmitters that help two-way communication between the gut and brain. Gut microbes digest fiber to produce lots of propionate, acetate, and butyrate. Propionate and acetate help moderate your appetite.

Butyrate helps repair your gut lining. This means that when there is a butyrate deficiency, your gut may be less repaired. This gives rise to the condition called leaky gut where foreign substances may leak pass the gut lining into the blood stream. This will cause autoimmune diseases and even autism.

Antibiotics can killed these beneficial bacteria. It takes up to two years to replenish your beneficial bacteria. Overuse of antibiotics has caused deadly infections. That's the reason why you must study natural alternative treatments to prevent the use of antibiotics.

Toxins are the primary cause of cancer and other diseases. So detoxing your body and avoiding taking carcinogenic substances found in foods, air, and water will reduce the risk of cancer. Man has created over 100,000 chemical compounds that are spewed or spilled into the soil, air, and water. You have to avoid taking them into your body.

One in four deaths is linked to air pollution. Pollutants found in the air are molds, bio-aerosols, combustion by-products, tobacco smoke, formaldehyde, arsenic, volatile organic compounds, phthalates, pesticides, asbestos, radon, and heavy metals like mercury and lead.

Your gut microorganisms make up 75% of your immunity system. Gut-related symptoms such as bloating, gas, pain, diarrhea, and constipation must never be treated lightly. Lack of biodiversity in your microbiome and too much bad bacteria may lead to chronic inflammation condition of the skin, joints, bowel, brain, and nervous system.

You can greatly reduce chronic inflammation by taking the following foods rich in Omega-3 fats, fermentation, high-fiber, polyphenols, and tryptophan:

Oily fish, olive oil, butter, ghee, yogurt, kefir, sauerkraut, cocoa, green tea, coffee, turkey, eggs, cheese, cooked potatoes, cooked plantain, cooked rice, beans, onions, ginger, garlic, leek, muesli, and unripe banana.

You can chelate and detox your body, fight diseases, and strengthen your immune system by taking the following foods, herbs, and supplements:

Coriander, parsley, broccoli, onions, ginger, garlic, leek, Brussel sprouts, kale, spinach, peas, chlorella, alpha lipoic acid, carnitine, apple cider vinegar, pre-biotics, pro-biotics, and pectin found in rinds of green apples, cabbage, banana, beet, and grapes.

You can cleanse your liver (your detox center) by taking the following foods:

Garlic, grapefruit, beetroot, onions, ginger, garlic, leek, lemon, green tea, avocado, turmeric, apple, walnut, broccoli, organ meat, cottage cheese, and butter.

By the way, 75% of your immunity comes from your gut. The remaining 25% comes from your lymphatic system, thymus, spleen, bone marrow, white blood cells, antibodies, and a complementary system comprising 30 proteins circulating in your blood stream that help antibodies fight infection.

Some people are sensitive to certain foods. This is usually due to the absence of a specific species of bacteria. So do keep tab of foods that may give you some digestive problems. Find alternatives to prevent such occurrences.

Do no harm

Staying healthy is very similar to sustaining a business. Your income must always be more than your expenses. Your assets must always be more than your liabilities. You must spend less than you earn.

In the same way, for you to stay healthy, you must keep your "expenses and liabilities" low.

Here are some of the dos and don'ts relating to chronic inflammation and all types of diseases:

- **Try to avoid medication**. Always search for natural alternative solutions to your health problems. Antibiotics kill your good gut bacteria. It takes two years to replenish them. Doctors will prescribe deadly drugs such as chemo drugs, brain drugs, Actos, NSAIDs, statins, Aricept, ACE inhibitors, pain relief and sleeping pills. They have serious side effects such as amyloid plaque formation, increased risks of heart attack, and even Alzheimer's disease. One ounce of prevention is far better than one ton of cure. A strong immune system is almost as good as vaccination. Your immunity can be weakened by stress, toxic wastes, nutrient deficiencies, sleep deprivation, and oxygen deprivation.

- **Beware of fake organic produce and farmer's market**. Soak and wash your fruits and vegetables in appropriate liquid such as baking soda and vegetable washing liquid. Give urban farming and country living ideas a try. Centenarians' favorite hobby is gardening. A smart alternative is to organize a community gardening project with subsidies from the government where you can participate in its activities including taking home fresh produce.

- **Don't breath in polluted air**. One in four deaths is due to air pollution. Use mask, air filtration system, or move to a cleaner place to live. Smoking is air pollution.

- **Don't drink polluted water. Don't buy bottled water.** Take control of your water supply by installing a flow filtration system. Alkaline water may not be useful. You need the filtration.

- **Avoid excessive drinking.** It will cause cancer and liver failure. Make appropriate lifestyle changes to reduce stress and improve energy management.

- **Avoid processed foods and drinks. Avoid sports and energy drinks.** They have too much sugar, additives, coloring, and preservatives which may cause insulin resistance and even pancreatic cancer. The inner surface of cans and packaging contain toxic substances. Eat whole foods.

- **Limit your intake of fried foods.** Foods cooked in high temperature produce carcinogenic substances such as acrylamide.
- **Avoid grilled and roasted meats.** They produce aromatic amines that cause cancer. Eating too much charred meat will lead to rectal cancer.
- **Reduce intake of meat.** Daily consumption of meat increases the risk prostate and colon cancer. Constipation makes matters worse. Eat more plant proteins.
- **Limit your intake of farm fish.** They contain more PCB and other toxins then wild fish.
- **Reduce your intake of salt and salted foods.** High acidic environment may encourage the proliferation of H. Pyloris and cancer. Reduce intake of cured meat. They contain a lot of nitrites which is carcinogenic.
- **Reduce intake of pickled foods.** Kimchi is good for you. But don't overdo it. Eating too much kimchi may lead to stomach cancer.
- **Never eat certain foods raw.** Cook certain foods like nightshades and cashew nuts thoroughly. They may contain toxins which must be neutralized by heat before you eat them.
- **Avoid taking artificial oils such as margarine.** Avoid trans fat that is found in hydrogenated oils. Limited intake of polyunsaturated oils such as vegetable oils because it contain excessive Omega-6 fatty acids.

P.S. Balance your intake of Omega-6 oils by taking more plant-based Omega-3 shorter-chain fatty acids (alpha-linolenic acid) found in plant oil such as walnut, soy, canola oil, flax seeds, and Chia seeds. Longer-chain Omega-3 fatty acids (EPA & DHA) are found in oily fish, krill, and shell fish. The ideal ratio of omega-6 to omega-3 fatty acids should be 1 to 1.

Remember that atherosclerosis is not caused by the amount of cholesterol carried by your LDP, but by oxidative damage of cell membranes caused by taking too much polyunsaturated fatty acids (PUFAs) and too little saturated fat.

Diets rich in EPA (eicosapentaenoic acid) reduce lipid and triglyceride levels in your blood, blood viscosity, platelet aggregation, risk of blood clot, and risk of heart attack.

10 high-fat foods that are actually good for you:

Avocado, cheese, dark chocolate, nuts, Chia seeds, coconut, coconut oil, extra virgin olive oil, fatty fish (salmon, trout, mackerel, sardines, herring), and whole eggs (don't eat it raw unless it is radiated).

Eat to beat disease

In his book, ***Eat To Beat Disease***, Dr. William Li shows how your body can heal itself. Your food can either be feeding or defeating disease.

Dr. William Li lists down 200 foods health-boosting foods that can starve cancer, reduce your risk of dementia, and beat dozens of avoidable diseases. They contain bioactive compounds that are as effective as expensive medication in beating disease. Several of your foods are:

Plums
Cinnamon
Jasmine tea
Red wine and beer
Black beans
San Marzano tomatoes
Olive oil
Cheeses like Jarlsberg, Camembert and cheddar
Sourdough bread

In his book, ***Lifespan: why we age and why we don't have to***, David Sinclair declares that aging is a disease and that disease can be treated. Once we know the science of aging, we can slow or even reverse aging.

Sinclair is a medical researcher that study aging at the molecular level. He discovered that a certain group of proteins called sirtuins stores molecular instructions in the aging process. As we age, these sirtuins decrease in number. Sinclair further discovered that the extent of DNA meythation determines fairly exactly how old you are biologically.

Additionally, Sinclair discovered that nicotinamide adenine dinucleotide (NAD) is the cofactor that is central to metabolism happening in our mitochondria.

Taking certain supplements could intervene in the metabolic processes of aging and slow down aging. On that basis, Sinclair is taking three supplements, namely:

- Nicotinamide mono-nucleotide (NMN) 1 g/daily in the morning
- Resveratol 1 g/daily with yogurt
- Metformin (a prescription drug for diabetes) 1 g/daily in the evening

Dr. Sinclair does not recommend that any one should follow his regiment. But that's what he does.

The New York Times asks you to think twice before taking an anti-aging pill like the diabetes drug metformin. It appears that metformin may blunt the health benefit of aerobic exercise in healthy older adults.

The side effect of metformin are diarrhea, nausea, vomiting, headache, and, sometimes, fatigue.

In other words, natural ways to stay healthy are always safer than pills and medication.

Intermittent Fasting

Intermittent fasting, also known as intermittent energy restriction, is an umbrella term for various meal timing schedules that cycle between voluntary fasting by reducing calorie intake and non-fasting over a given period.

Intermittent fasting is not recommended for growing children, teenagers, pregnant women, competitive athletes, patients, and the elderly.

For most people, meal scheduling based on time restriction is the safest and least disruptive. For healthy adults, you need to skip breakfast and delay taking your lunch as long as you can. At any time, you can drink warm filtered water. You can then eat healthy snacks such as milk with dates, salad using fruits and vegetable with DIY salad dressing. Dark chocolate with yogurt, sweet potatoes and similar dishes can all be used as snacks.

Intermittent fasting is superior to simple calorie restriction because the latter does not allow your body to cleanse itself. When you fast, your body goes into a starvation mode which triggers a response of increasing human growth hormone production, increasing stem cell production, cleaning up dead or sickly cells, and flushing them out of your body.

For the highest level of health, fitness, and vitality, commit yourself to do ALL of the following strategies:

- Intermittent fasting
- High intensity interval training
- Strength & flexibility training
- Quality sleep
- Recommended supplements (NMN, resveratol, CoQ10, a-lipoic aicd, acetyl-l-carnitine, n-acetyl cysteine, vitamin B, C3, E, and K2, krill oil...)
- Diet with pre-biotics, probiotics, plenty of fruits, vegetables, nuts and healthy fats.; no processed foods; no toxic cosmetics, clean air and so forth.
- Stress management based on professionalism, the beliefs of greatness and the wise definition of success.

Mitochondria

What are mitochondria?

Mitochondria are microscopic organelles in your cells outside the nucleus. Every human cell contains anywhere from 1,000 to 2,500 mitochondria.

Its main function is to produce molecules known as adenosine triphosphate (ATP) to generate energy for you to stay alive. ATP cannot be stored. Therefore ATP production must occur continuously through our life.

How much ATP does the mitochondria produce every day?

A healthy person at rest produces his body weight in ATP every day. This works out to 300 grams of ATP per minute. When you exercise, your ATP production goes up to a maximum around 1 kilogram per minute.

Because many parts of ATP will be recycle, we don't bloat up in size. The chief elements and compounds in the metabolic processes inside mitochondria are hydrogen, carbon, oxygen, sulfur, coenzyme Q, niacin, and many others.

Factors that will damage mitochondria are:

Oxidants leaked while producing ATP
Oxidative damage to DNA (aging)
Genome weakness
Toxic metals
Pollutants
Prescription drugs
Alcohol

When your mitochondria malfunction, the following diseases will be aggravated:

Early aging
Amyotrophic lateral sclerosis
Alzheimer's disease
Autism
Cardiovascular disease
Chronic fatigue syndrome
Dementia

Diabetes
Huntington's disease
Migraine headache
Parkinson's disease

Supplements that may support mitochondria function are:

- CoQ10 + vitamin E
- A-Lipoic acid + acetyl-l-carnitine
- N-acetyl cysteine

Stem cells

What are stem cells?

Stem cells are cells that can differentiate into other types of cells and also divided in self-renewal to produce more of the same type of stem cells.

Embryology is the branch of biology that studies the prenatal development of sex cells (gametes), fertilization, and development of embryos and fetuses. Embryology also encompasses the study of congenital disorders that occur before birth known as teratology.

In humans, embryo refers to the ball of dividing cells from the moment the fertilized egg (zygote) implants itself in the uterus wall until the eighth week after conception. Beyond the eight week after conception, it is no longer called an embryo but a fetus, with observable features of differentiated cells.

In human adults, stem cells still remain, located chiefly in bone marrow, adipose tissues and blood. In 2012, Sir John B Gurdon and Shinya Yamanaka were awarded the Nobel Prize in Physiology or Medicine for the discovery that mature cells can be reprogrammed to become pluripotent.

While various therapies are being developed using stem cells, they carry moderate to high risks, and cost tens of thousands of dollars. Several patients were nearly blind after getting a stem cell treatment.

The US Food & Drug Administration (FDA) has started investigating clinics that are offering stem cell therapies, calling such clinics "unscrupulous clinics" selling "so-called cures." The FDA seized materials from one clinic, StemImmune Inc in San Diego, California, and sent a warning letter to another clinic in Florida.

Your body has the capacity to produce sufficient stem cells for tissue repair. But this activity can be reduced by unhealthy lifestyle choices such as high caloric intake, high intake of sugar and salt, and excess deep belly fat surrounding your internal organs.

If that is true, then lowering your caloric intake, reducing your intake of sugar hidden away into the ingredients of processed foods, exercise, and fasting, will boost the supply of your stem cells.

Stress management

There are thousands of mutations happening in our body. Then why are we not sick?

It is because our body's immune system can deal with them effectively.

If this is so, it follows that when our immune system weakens, then disease will follow.

How do we keep our immune system strong and healthy?

By leading a healthy lifestyle.

What is a healthy lifestyle?

A healthy lifestyle is a way of life that helps preserve and enhance the greatest asset you have - you and your body, mind, and soul.

You have four dimensions to take care of - physical, social-emotional, mental, and spiritual. Man does not live by bread alone but by pursuing a cause greater than himself.

You take care of your physical dimension by exercising, proper nutrition, and stress management.

You take care of your social-emotional dimension by service, empathy, synergy, and internal security.

You take care of your mental dimension by reading, visualizing your goals and dream, planning, and writing.

You take care of your spiritual dimension by reflection, clarification of your principles, values, and virtues, meditation and prayer.

Studies have shown that a man is most happy when he is about to retire. The first year of retirement is filled with many things he had missed doing - lazing in the beach, take long trips, playing golf everyday and so forth.

Studies have shown that by the second or third year, things start to get boring and less meaningful. Then for the first time, he begin to appreciate his work life, where most of his friends are. That's when lifestyle becomes so important.

A daily schedule of work and play continues to be important. In retirement, you'll be bored and sad to stop working entirely. You begin to feel useless, unwanted. Serving others need not be sacrificial. You are serving your own well-being as you serve others.

The main difference when you retire is that you don't have to race around at top speed. You can pace yourself better during retirement.

Most adults live unhealthy lifestyles. They put their lives at risk. Studies have shown that chronic stress can accelerate the spread of cancer, and increase the seriousness of a health condition.

Chronic stress can cause people to make these six unhealthy lifestyle choices:

- **Exercise less.** Exercise takes time and discipline. A stressful work life usually means rushing around, taking no breaks, missing meals, and long working hours. As a result your exercise less. Exercise helps to improve blood circulation, improve muscle tone, improve your mood by releasing feel-good biochemicals called endorphins, thus protecting you from cardiovascular diseases.
- **Eat junk food.** When you are over-stressed, you'll go for your comfort foods which are usually unhealthy, full of sugar, salt, and preservatives. When you are not stressed, then you are more prepared to make healthier choices, swapping fast foods and cakes for lean meats, nuts, fruits, and vegetables.
- **Sleep less**. If you are still thinking and worried about your work at dinner time, its going to give you indigestion and a disturbed sleep. You'll also be sleeping less, turning and tossing in your sleep. Sleep debt is an often-overlooked factor in causing heart diseases.
- **Stay plugged in**. There is a strong myth that watching TV is a great way to destress. It is true if you select movies or programs that calm you down rather then scramble your emotions. Healthier choices include reading, listening to music, taking a hot shower, exercising, dancing, and singing.
- **Smoke.** TV commercials and bad examples around us brainwash us into thinking that smoking will calm our nerves and

make us think better. Smoking is unhealthy because it deprives your lungs of oxygen which is essential to many body functions. Smoking accelerates plaque formation in your arteries. This will increase the risk of blood clot jamming in your blood vessels, increasing the risk of stroke or heart attack.

- **Drink alcohol.** Here again, we have been brainwashed by TV commercials and bad examples around us that drinking alcohol will help us forget our problems. Alcohol will kill liver cells leading to other health problems. Drinking wine and beer in the right amount can have health benefits. Health tonic usually come in a bottle with a very small glass specifically to limit your intake. The limit for wine should be a quarter glass a day. The upper limit of beer should be one small can.

In their book, ***The Power of Full Engagement***, Jin Loehr & Tony Schwartz reveal that managing energy, not time, is the key to high performance and personal renewal. They will show you many ways of boosting your productivity.

Taking a five-minute break every hour increases your work productivity. During this break, you can choose to do several things - get out from your chair and move around, wash your face, brush your teeth, have a cup of hot or cold drink, chat with your friends, do a quick breathing exercise like a Zen master and so forth. You can also simply close your eyes, massage your eyes gently, and meditate.

Centenarians' favorite hobby

One of the best ways to lead a less stressful life, and still attain your financial goals, is to consider healthy alternative to city living. With Internet connection and e-commerce businesses, you can liberate yourself from any fixed location.

In her book, ***The Encyclopedia of Country Living:*** *the original manual for living off the land & doing it yourself*, Carla Emery, will show how you can take a mini vacation away from the urban jungle. The only draw back is that it is more than 900 pages thick, and the paper is rather thin, probably to bring down the cost as well as the weight of the book.

However, if you don't mind having the book, you don't have to read it from cover to cover, but go straight to any chapter that covers your favorite hobby.

Alternative you may like to subscribe to the free newsletter from ***Mother Earth News.*** They are dedicated to conserving our planet's natural resources while helping you to conserve your financial resources. It is an excellent way of life when the financial system around the world collapses.

Studies show that gardening is the most common hobby among centenarians around the world. Studies have also shown that farmers are one-third less likely to have a chronic illness than non-farmers.

Growing your own food has many rewards such as these:

- It teaches you patience, thus lowering your stress level.
- You get fresher and uncontaminated nutrient-dense produce.
- It saves you money cutting down on your grocery bill.
- It gives you plenty of sunshine, fresh air and exercise.
- You'll get exposure to beneficial soil microbes that will improve your microbiome.
- You'll get more social contact and camaraderie especially if it is a community garden.
- You can age in place.

If you are living in an urban area, you can still do gardening in small spaces. You may like to check out ***The Edible Balcony*** by Alex Mitchell.

While physical well-being is important in living longer, it is our farmer's sense of flowing with nature that is even more important. That's why, for example, that Italy's oldest people who drink and smoke still live extra-long lives.

The Cilento region of southern Italy is home to a unique group of people. In the rural villages of the area, between the mountains and the Mediterranean coast lives a particularly remarkable group of people.

They spend their days outdoors, eating fish, smoking cigarettes, and drinking wine. Many of them are overweight. There are some seemingly unhealthy habits out there. But many of them live way pass 90.

Their Mediterranean diet certainly plays a part. Their good genes also play a part. Researchers discovered that a handful of psychological traits play a significant part in their longevity.

Exceptional longevity is characterized by a balance between acceptance of adversities and a grit to overcome adversities, a positive and optimistic attitude, and close ties to family, religion, and land, providing purpose in life.

The oldest among them exhibit high levels of mental well-being, with low levels of depression and anxiety. They are all rooted in their sense of purpose, responsibility, and a healthy relationship with their natural surroundings.

Exercise

What is exercise?

Exercise is physical activity that is planned, structured, and repetitive for the purpose of conditioning any part of the body. Exercise improves your health and fitness.

The World Health Organization (WHO) recommend that you do at least 150 minutes of moderate physical activity per week. So if you exercise three times a week, that works out to 50 minutes per session.

Moderate physical activity means raising your heart rate to 50 to 70% of your maximum heart rate. A rough estimate of your maximum heart rate is 220 minus your age).

Vigorous physical activity means raising your heart rate to 70 to 85% of your maximum heart rate.

There is another more complicated way of measuring your exercise intensity and that is to measure your metabolic equivalent or MET. You need not bother with it if you like, unless you are in competitive sports.

You can start by using a mobile app that counts your steps. - such as Argus, Fitbit, and Moves. This method requires the least commitment. If you run or cycle, you can also use mobile apps to track your activity.

If you like, you may step up and consider buying a fitness tracker that you can wear on your wrist. It costs at least $50 and can go beyond $250. The more features you need , the more you have to spend on a fitness trackers. There are built-in features like heart rate monitor, GPS, distance traveled, and even in-depth sleep analysis. For swimmers, you may ask for a waterproof fitness tracker.

The Cooper 2.4 km (1.5 miles) run test is a simple running test of aerobic fitness. It requires only a stopwatch and a running track. This is the alternative to the Cooper 12-minute run test.

A good fitness level is taking 12 minutes to run 2.4 km for males, and 15 minutes for females.

In his book, ***Spark**: the revolutionary new science of exercise and the brain*, John J Ratey show that you can beat stress, lift your mood, fight memory loss, sharpen your intellect, and improve your work performance simply by elevating your heart rate and break a sweat.

Aerobic exercise physically remodel your brain for peak performance. Endurance exercise increases a metabolic hormone called fibroblast growth factor 21. Strength training decreases another metabolic hormone called fibroblast growth factor 10. In other words, different types of exercise affect your metabolism differently.

Once you have this level of fitness, you may go for the top level of fitness and longevity - high intensity interval exercises. The rule is that the higher your exercise intensity, the shorter the time you need to do the exercise. A 4-minute high intensity interval training (HIIT), for example is equivalent to 60 minutes of moderate exercise.

Studies have shown that intensity exercises produces more post-exercise oxygen consumption than endurance exercises. When a person works out at intensity, they can't sustain for a long period of time. This is because there is an oxygen deficit and also a rapid build up of lactic acid in the muscles.

There are two additional benefits of high intensity exercise. The first benefit is called after-burn. This is when your body continues to burn fat after the exercise. The second benefit is that it will improve your body's capacity to use oxygen for energy. The experts calls it VO2 max.

Studies have shown that the best health results comes from a run to rest ratio of 2:1. For example, you run at your top speed for 60 seconds and rest for 30 seconds, and then repeat this, say, 7 times. This means that the time taken for this exercise is 7 times 1.5 minutes, or around 10.5 minutes. If you add ten minutes for warming up at the start of the exercise and ten minutes of stretching at the end of the exercise, the grand total time taken for the exercise proper is 30.5 minutes.

For variety, you may like to consider other forms of exercises that can complement your aerobic exercises. This will include racket sports, golf, cycling, swimming, Qigong and yoga.

Sleep

Sleep is one of the most powerful way to stay healthy. This factor is often overlooked.

Quality sleep can reduce the risk of Alzheimer's. Deep sleep is essential for waste removal and body repair, rebuilding cartilage of your knee joints, nervous system repair, and maintaining metabolic homeostasis.

In his book, ***Why We Sleep****: unlocking the power of sleep and dreams,* Matthew Walker reveals the transformative power of sleep. Sleep is one of the most important but least understood aspect of our life, wellness, and longevity. We suffer devastating health consequences when we don't sleep well.

Here are the tips to get more quality sleep:

- **Fixed time.** Always try to go to sleep at the same time each night and get up at the same time each morning. The circadian clock in your brain is set at 2100 hrs at night and 0500 hrs in the morning.
- **No naps after 1500 hrs.** Try to nap before 1500 hrs and don't make it too long - less than one hour.
- **No heavy meal** three hours before bedtime. A light snack is

all right.

- **No caffeine and alcohol** after 1800 hrs. The caffeine and alcohol will stay in your system for more than three hours unless you exercise.
- **Avoid nicotine completely.** It will damage your throat, voice box and your lungs. This may lead to lung infection and asthma. Coughing will disturb your sleep.
- **Exercise regularly.** Exercise will flush out your waste through seat, flush your skin, and tire you. This will prepare you for quality sleep.
- **Comfort.** Make your room, quiet, dark, comfortable, and temperature set at around 24 degree Celsius.. You may like to install an air filter to eliminate dust, pollen, odors and so forth. If you can afford it, soundproof your bedroom. To cut out light, you may like to put on a eye shade, especially for your afternoon nap.
- **Lulling to sleep**. Discover what is the best way for you to fall asleep, such as listening to soft music, reading a light-hearted novel, and so forth.
- **Take a sleep aid.** There are several natural sleep aids in the market that are backed by science. To ensure its continued effectiveness, you may switch supplement every six months or so. They usually contain melatonin, valerian root, magnesium, lavender, passion flower, glycine, tryptophan, ginkgo biloba, L-theanine, and kava.

Urinary incontinence

Even though we should try to prevent diseases such as cardiovascular diseases, diabetes, and cancer, we must make an extra effort to prevent urinary incontinence because it is the most messy and irritating condition to be in.

Urinary incontinence can be caused by stress, urge, overflow, and aging.

Urinary incontinence happens because of the following factors:

Weak bladder muscle
Weak pelvic floor muscles
Nerve damage
Constipation
Enlarged prostate
Enlarged colon
Blocked urethra due to tumors or an enlarged prostate.

Getting a diagnosis and treatment from your doctor for urinary incontinence can be very frustrating, invasive, and painful. It may require attachment of objects, medication and surgery.

There is no question that one ounce of prevention is far better than one ton of cure. While you are still young, maintain your current level of health. Don't lose your muscle tone. Make healthier choices like regular exercise, have quality sleep, manage your stress and improve your relationship.

In this way you will delay the onset of this condition until you are 80.

So here are a few way to help you prevent or mitigate urinary incontinence:

Strengthen bladder muscles. Learn to delay urination after you have the urge to go. You may start with delaying it for ten minutes.

Double voiding. You urinate once, wait for a few minutes and then urinate again.

Fluid and diet management. Alcohol, caffeine and acidic foods tends to make you urinate more. Reducing excessive fluid intake will also help. Weight management is important.. Improving muscle tone by daily exercise will certain mitigate your urinary incontinence.

Pelvic floor muscle exercises. These are also known as Kegel exercises. Contract the muscles that stops urinating and hold it for 2 seconds. Relax for 3 seconds. Then repeat this set several time. Increase the holding time and do it until your muscle is much stronger.

Treat causes of urinary incontinence. Causes of urinary incontinence may be enlarged prostrate, enlarged colon, constipation, and blocked urethra. When you treat the underlying causes, your urinary incontinence will be less burdensome.

Knee arthroscopy

Your mobility depends on the condition of your knee joints. When you have difficulty in walking, then you may need a wheelchair. This will definitely lower your quality of life. So take good care of your knee joints.

Your knee joints are the most remarkable structures.

The pressure on your knee joints can go up to four times your body weight. This means that if you weigh 150 lbs, your knee joints has to take 600 lbs of pressure when you are running.

That is why your thigh bone (femur) and leg bone (tibia) are capped with cartilage to protect your bone endings and for mobility. Cartilage is a combination of proteins and sugar that can take this kind of pressure.

A ligament is a tough tissue that connect one bone to another bone. There are four major ligaments that support your knee. The two ligaments on the sides of your knee joint are called medial collateral ligament and lateral collateral ligament. The anterior cruciate ligament runs in front of your knee joint. The posterior cruciate ligament runs on the back of your knee joint.

The other hard tissues you have in your knee joints are the many tendons. A tendon is the hard tissue at the ending of your thigh and leg muscles that attaches to your thigh and leg bones.

The narrow space between the endings of you thigh bone and the leg bone is filled with synovial fluid which contain hyaluronic acid.

Each knee joint has two curved cartilage called the meniscus that act as a shock absorber. The meniscus can be damaged by twisting movements that force the knee beyond its normal range of movement. This occurs during games like football, basketball, running, jogging, tennis and so forth. This risk is higher when the knee joint show some arthritic degenerative changes.

The traditional method of opening up the knee is by incision. A better method is called knee arthroscopy. Here, one tiny hole is made on either side of the knee for microscopic inspection and surgery.

Try to avoid doing knee surgery. Cartilage, ligaments and tendons, can heal provided the building materials are there and give it a period of protected rest:

- **Reduce inflammation** and detox your body taking these bioactive compounds - proteolytic enzymes, kiwi fruit, ginger, asparagus, sauerkraut, kimchi, Indian frankinsence, citrus bioflavonoids, hibiscus, Chinese skullcap and so forth.
- **Pain relief** comes from such ingredients as MSM (methyl-sufonyl-methane), bromelain and papan.
- **Cartilage building material** comes from Type II collagen.

- **Avoid factors that can destroy the collagen** in your body: poor sleep, excess sugar consumption, high stress that release too much cortisol, overexposure to the sun, low intake of anti-oxidants, lack of exercise, poor gut health, nutrient deficiencies, and free radicals.

Blindness

Our vision is one of our most precious senses.

Most people have eye problems at one time or another. Some are minor and will go away on their own, or are easy to treat at home. Others need the attention of an eye specialist.

Here are the eye problems you should be aware of:

Red eye. The surface of your eye has many tiny blood vessels more properly called capillaries. When there is infection or irritation, they expand and thus appear red. Red eye may be accompanied by excessive tearing. Eyestrain can also have similar effect for reading too long without sufficient break.

Another cause of red eye is actually a bursting of one capillary. It look frightening, but it will clear when you drip several eye drops on your eye.

Night blindness. When your vision fails you at night, it may indicate nutrient deficiency, nearsightedness, cataracts, or keratoconus.

Lazy eye. Lazy eye or amblyopia occur in one eye because it is less developed than the other eye. This condition should be treat during early childhood.

Cross eyes. You are suffering from cross eyes when both eye movements are not synchronize. You need and eye specialist to correct this condition.

Colorblindness. When you are not able to distinguish reds and greens, you are colorblind. This happen when the cones in your eyes are not working or are absent. This condition cannot be treated. However, there are special contact lenses and glasses to help people differentiate between colors.

Uveitus. Uveitis is a group of diseases that is due to the inflammation of the middle layer of your eye that contain the most capillaries. Uveitis is caused by other diseases such as AIDS, rheumatoid arthritis, and ulcerative colitis.

Presbyopia. This is an eye condition in which you can see objects clearly but cannot do so for objects within reading distance. This can be treated with reading glasses, contact lenses, Lasik, and other eye surgery.

Floaters. This is an eye condition in which you can see tiny specks floating across your vision. They can be harmless. But it can also indicate something more serious such as retina detachment.

Dry eyes. This is an eye condition when your eyes are dry because your eyes do not producing enough tears. Sometimes it is due to a very dry air in the room. In this case you may need to use a humidifier. Otherwise, you may need special eye drops.

Cataracts. This is an eye condition when a portion of your eye lens turns cloudy. If the cloudy portion stays small, then it is not serious. But if it progresses quickly, you need to rush to see an eye specialist.

Glaucoma. This eye condition occur when there is a small difference between the pressure inside the eyeball and outside, leading to a slight bulge in the eye ball. It happens when there is an injury to the eye, a block blood vessel, and inflammation of the eye.

Retinal disorders. Retina is an inner layer of the eye that connects to the brain via the optic nerve. It collects images and pass it on to the brain. A portion of the retina called the macula controls your central vision. Your macula may be degenerating due to old age. Diabetes may also cause damage to the capillaries in your retina. A small portion of your retina may also get detached from the layer underneath.

Conjunctivitis. This is an eye condition in which the conjunctiva is inflamed. It may be due to infection, exposure to chemical, and an allergic reaction.

Corneal diseases. This is an eye condition in which your cornea is caused by injury, infection, and chemical. This may be treated by a new prescription lenses, medicated eye drops, and sometimes surgery.

Eyelid problems. This is an eye condition in which the inner lining of your eye lid may similarly be affected by injury, infection, and chemical. This can be treated by washing, medication, or surgery.

Here are the many natural ways to improve your vision:

If you pay attention to Dr. David Sinclair, you'll get all the tips on longevity. His daily supplements are NMN, resveratol, and Metformin. I suggest you may take NMN and resveratol but not Metformin.

If you pay attention to Dr. William Li too, you'll know how to eat to beat disease. Many of the diseases will affect your eyes. Dr. William Li has a list of 200 foods that will provide all the bioactive compounds to beat diseases.

Vitamin A, C, and E, zinc, and other minerals can help prevent macula degeneration. There are present in such foods as carrots, red peppers, broccoli, spinach, strawberries, sweet potatoes, and all citrus fruits.

Lutein and zeaxanthin may be taken in larger doses in supplement form. All the other lifestyle activities such as stress management, sleep, exercise, and lots of sunshine will all support better vision.

Reduce your intake of saturated fats and take more healthy Omega-3 fatty acids.

You may eat grass-fed beef occasionally. You can get most of your protein from plants.

Reducing inflammation is also very important to have better vision. So you have to avoid processed foods, excessive sodium chloride intake, alcohol, smoke, deep fried and BBQ foods.

Master the art of using pre-biotics and pro-biotics. All health and all diseases comes from your gut. The billions of good bacteria gives you 75% of your immunity power to fight mutation in cells and all alien organisms.

Don't waste time on some doctor's recommendations about regular checkups and tests. Why? Because these deal with symptoms. The cause of diseases is lifestyle activities. Therefore, spend more time in ticking your checklist of your lifestyle activities, what you should do and what you should not do.

When you do that, the magic will automatically happen - your blood sugar will be balanced, your blood pressure will be healthy, your cholesterol levels will be of no concern, your arteries will remain unclogged, and so forth.

Last but not least, protect your eyes by not rubbing your eyes with dirty hands. Wash your hands regularly. Wear protective eyewear or goggles to protect your eyes from injury, sparks, chemicals, or harmful light rays.

And remember to take five-minute breaks every hour when

using your eyes for reading, working on your computer and so forth. Not only ill you protect your vision. It will boost your productivity.

Act now on your beliefs

Remember that doctors as a group is the third leading cause of death. So don't treat doctors like gods. They make mistakes just like you and me. Control your destiny or someone else will. Take charge of your life by doing your own independent thinking and research.

Practice healthy living, and avoid the first medication at all cost, except in emergency cases such as food poisoning, injuries with excessive bleeding and so forth.

FBI will tell you that white collar criminals are very charming people. Vote for a national leader who can really fight corruption in the health and all the other sectors.

World Health Organization (WHO) has a medicine watchdog in its Department of Essential Medicines and Health Products (EMP).

The EMP contributes to strengthening health systems by providing support to countries in improving access to and the use of safe, effective, and quality assured medicines.

EMP develops and updates norms and standards and the provision of technical support. 80% of deaths in poor and middle-income countries are due to poor accessibility to medicines.

You can reach EMP at www.who.int/medicines

Decisions have the power to steer and change your life forever. Therefore, nothing affects the quality of your life than your ability to make the right decisions. All that you have achieved or failed to achieved can be traced back to the decisions you've made - on issues concerning your vote, health, wealth, relationships, and life purpose.

Change your beliefs, and you will change your principles, values, virtues, habits, attitudes, social skills, ethics, behavior and so forth.

In life there are no mistakes, only lessons. The secret to resilience, happiness and a less stressful success is to avoid focusing on stagnant traits. Instead, focus on adopting an active, growth-oriented and problem-solving approach to life, and enjoying the journey together with your loved ones.

Here are the beliefs of greatness that will empower you to enjoy the journey with your loved ones:

- That which is hateful to you, do not do to your fellow human beings. Any interpretation of scriptures that bred hatred or disdain for others - whatever their beliefs - was illegitimate. (Hillel)
- True religion is protecting the powerless - orphans, widows, homeless, migrant workers, disabled, and injured soldiers returning from an unnecessary war.
- Power without love is reckless and abusive. Love without power is sentimental and anemic. Power at its best is love implementing the demands of justice. Justice at its best is power correcting everything that stands against love. (Martin Luther King)
- That which matter most must never be at the mercy of things that matter least. (Goethe)
- Courage is not the absence of fear but rather the judgment that something is more important than fear. The brave may not live forever. But the cautious do not live at all. (Meg

Cabot)

- So long as you open your heart to beauty, hope, cheer, courage and power, so long are you young. (Samuel Ulman). I know of no more encouraging fact than the unquestionable ability of man to elevate his life by conscious endeavor (Henry David Thoreau).
- We should encourage each other to follow the rules of considerate conduct such as think before we act, listen more, argue less, seek first to understand, think twice before asking favors, avoid shifting responsibility and blame, avoid jumping to conclusions, respect other's opinion, and enjoying the journey with your loved ones.
- If you want to achieve what you've never achieved before, you have to grow to become what you've never become before. (Brian Tracy). Insanity is doing the same over and over again and expecting different results. No problem can be solved at the same level of consciousness that created it. (Albert Einstein)
- Success and cheerfulness in life are not the result of what we have but rather how we live. What we do with the things we already have now makes the biggest difference in the quality of our life. (Tony Robbins)
- Studies have shown that companies hire for attitude and train for skills. (Singapore Airlines).
- Humility is the beginning of wisdom. (Zen habits)
- A foolish definition of success is the attainment of a certain amount of money, power, and privilege. A wise definition of success is enjoying the journey of lifelong learning with your loved ones.
- All men are created equal, endowed with the unalienable rights to life, liberty and the pursuit of happiness. (US Dec-

laration of Independence)

- The world will be safer and prosperous when all nations adhere to the principles of peaceful coexistence where there is mutual respect for each other's territorial sovereignty and the right to self-determination and non-interference. (China-India)

- Whether a cat is black or white makes no difference. A cat that catches mice is a good cat. Whether we label an ideology socialism, capitalism, communism, or authoritarianism makes no difference. A government that can provide affordable subsidized public housing, meaningful jobs, efficient transport system, clean environment, fantastic schools, universal health care, recreation centers, and national security is a good government and should be given a strong mandate to govern. (Deng Xiaoping)

- Every nation must strive to avoid contracting the national disease of schizophrenia where there are two equally dominant sectarian political parties, bickering with each other like two juveniles. It is best if there is a political party that promote universal values that protect the rights of minorities so as to gain at least 70% of popular vote thus attaining a strong mandate to govern.

- Workers must enjoy democracy at the workplace where they have a say in the management of the company and reserve the right to buy the company if the owners decide to sell.

- All citizens must have a fair share in the prosperity of the nation. This can be achieved by practicing universal basic income (UBI) calculated as a small percentage of the living wage. UBI is able to soften the ills of neoliberalism by reducing the pain and frustration of the underprivileged who are the victims of the wealth gap between the rich and the poor. UBI is able to reduce the risk of violent civil unrest.

- Every citizen must be given universal healthcare.
- Every person has the right to demand privacy, especially when he or she has not committed any crime. (Edward Snowden)
- Every person has the right to choose his own way of life without being judged or criticized so long as he or she respects the rule of law. He can choose voluntary simplicity, country living, living off the grid, any profession, urban competition, climbing the corporate ladder, activism, the military, or politics.
- Whistleblowers should be protected by law when they expose the wrongdoings within the company or government.

Chapter ten

CYBER INSECURITY

**rtificial intelligence: it will kill us."**

That's the title of a TED Talk given by US defense expert Jay Tuck.

Jay Tuck begins:

The subject of my talk is about something that is smarter than you are: artificial intelligence.

In fact, a lot of people who work in artificial intelligence believe that artificial intelligence is a thousand times smarter than we are. It will be moving at speeds that is a hundred thousand times as fast as we think, and it will be digesting information and data a million times more than we can.

Artificial intelligence is a software that writes itself. It writes its own updates. It renews itself.

We used to think of software as stuff that we create and control. But now its far more advanced than that. It is now not simple software. It is almost alive. It writes independently, autonomously, and it develops its own way of thinking and there are dangers associated with so much power.

This is not science fiction any more. AI is already smarter, faster, and more autonomous than us many times. For example, in the stock markets in New York, London, Tokyo or Frankfurt, the people working there are just like movie extras. It is the supercomputers who are doing all the billion-dollar business in milliseconds. Super computers are in the center of our financial system.

These high-frequency computers have far exceeded what human beings can do. Super computers are also in the center of our transport and communication systems. Your bookings for hotel, airline tickets, and land transport are done by them in milliseconds.

In the life and death business of medicine, super computers are in the thick of things. They can recognize a tumor on a MRT or a CT faster, better, and more precisely than the best radiologists in the world.

The more chilling thing is that such super computers can be given warm skin, fragrance, and features like a human. But they don't have a warm blood circulatory system. They have cold code lines.

We used to think of surveillance as one camera and one person. But now artificial intelligence allow us to take pictures that covers an area of 15 square miles from our satellite 17,500 feet away. We can instantly zoom in to view people walking on the streets.

The super computer ARGUS-IS can take videos from its 368 chips to create a 1.8 billion pixel video stream. It can produce a million terabytes of data every day. All these data can be fed into an AI brain that can analyze everybody captured in its data bank.

Drones can go into enemy territory and drop sensor packages the size of tennis balls to do many recordings - audio, visual, seismic, chemical, and radioactivity. Artificial intelligence can fuse all these data and make sense of them - such as the kind of vehicles they're using, what kind of troop movements are there, what are they transporting, whether they are radioactive and so forth.

In the US, we have the Defense Advanced Research Projects Agency (DARPA) that coordinates the acquisitions of stakes in some of the most powerful, influential corporations and operation units in the world - Google, Lockheed Martin and units in the Navy. In other words, all these factors are networked like the Internet of Things.

Studies have shown that AI robots make less mistakes than human beings. They are therefore equipped to make decisions including a kill decision. It is made indestructible by having thousands of backups in many computer programs so that if parts of the network is destroyed, it will continue to operate.

Glenn Greenwald

Glenn Edward Greenwald, born March 6, 1967, is an American journalist and author.

Greenwald received his BA degree in Philosophy from George Washington University in 1990, and a JD degree from New York University School of Law in 1994.

Greenwald practiced law in the litigation Department at Wachtell, Lipton Rosen & Katz (1994 - 1995). He then co-founded his own litigation firm called Greenwald Christoph & Holland, which was later renamed Greenwald Christoph PC, where he litigated cases concerning issues of US constitutional law and civil rights.

In 2003, Greenwald got bored with law and decided do other things that were more engaging including political writing. He began his blog ***Unclaimed Territory***, focusing on the investigation pertaining to the Plame affair, the CIA leak grand jury investigation, the federal indictment of Scooter Libby, and the NSA warrantless surveillance (2001 to 2007) controversy.

Greenwald wrote his first book, ***How Would a Patriot Act? Defending American values from a president run amok.***

Greenwald was described as the American left most fearless political commentator. He joined Britain's ***The Guardian*** newspaper, contributing a weekly column and a daily blog from 2012. In 2013, Greenwald reported on the top-secret US Foreign Intelligence Surveillance Court order requiring Verizon to provide the National Security Agency (NSA) with telephone metadata for all calls between the US and abroad, as well as all domestic calls.

On October 15, 2013, Greenwald announced that he was going to leave ***The Guardian*** to start along with his colleagues Laura Poitras and Jeremy Scahill, a media organization called ***First Look Media,*** launching its first online publication called ***The Intercept.***

Julian Assange

Julian Paul Assange, born 3 July 1971, is an Australian editor, publisher, and activist who founded ***Wikileaks*** in 2006.

Wikileaks came to international attention in 2010 when it published a series of leaks provided by Chelsea Manning. These leaks included the Collateral Murder video (April 2010), the Afghanistan war logs (July 2010), the Iran war logs (October 2010), and CableGate (November 2010).

After the 2010 leaks, the US government launched a criminal investigation into ***Wikileaks.***

In November 2010, Sweden issued an international arrest warrant for Assange on a charge of sexual assault. Assange denied the allegations, claiming that these were just a pretext for him to be extradited to the US.

On 7 December 2010, Assange surrendered to the UK police. He was released on bail within ten days. Assange breached his bail of 340,000 pounds and sought asylum in Ecuador., first remaining in the Embassy of Ecuador in London for eight years.

Edward Snowden

Edward Joseph Snowden, born June 21, 1983, in Elizabeth City, North Carolina. He passed the GED test without finishing high school. He attended Anne Arundel College. He also did not finish college but worked online toward a Master's degree at the University of Liverpool, England in 2011.

Snowden was interested in Japanese popular culture, so he studied the Japanese language. He worked for an anime company that had a resident office in the US. He also studied Mandarin Chinese and was deeply interested in martial arts.

Snowden was an agnostic, but could not find this category in a military recruitment form. So he ticked "Buddhism" as his religion. He enlisted in the US Army Reserve on May 7, 2004 and became a Special Forces candidate through its 18X enlistment option. He broke both legs during training and was discharged on September 28, 2004.

Snowden worked for less than a year in 2005 as a security guard at the University of Maryland's Center for Advanced Study of Language, a research center sponsored by the National Security Agency (NSA)

AT a 2006 job-fair focused on intelligence agencies, Snowden accepted an offer for a position at the CIA. The Agency assigned him to the global communication division at CIA headquarters in Langley, Virginia.

Snowden was a computer wizard and so was sent to the CIA secret school for technology specialists, where he lived in a hotel for six months while studying and training full-time.

In March 2007, the CIA stationed Snowden with diplomatic cover in Geneva, Switzerland. He was responsible for maintaining computer network security. The CIA hand-picked Snowden to support the US president at the 2008 NATO summit in Romania. In February 2009, Snowden resigned from the CIA.

Snowden soon joined Dell which manages computer systems for multiple government agencies. Snowden was assigned to a NSA facility in Yokota Air Base near Tokyo. His job was to instruct top officials and military officers on how to defend their networks against Chinese hackers. He rose through the ranks in Dell and soon became a cyber strategist and an expert in cyber counterintelligence at several US locations.

At this time, Snowden watched on TV how the NSA Director James Clapper lied on oath to Congress. He became disillusioned by what the US government was doing.

In March 2013, Dell reassigned Snowden to Hawaii as lead technologist for the NSA's information-sharing office in the employment of Booz Allen. Before he left Japan, he copied more than 50,000 documents.

Snowden had read Greenwald's article in ***The Washington Post*** detailing how Poitras's controversial films had made her a target of the US government. Snowden decided to leak to Gellman of ***The Washington Post***. Gellman could not promise to publish within 72 hours. So Snowden decided to leak to Greenwald and Poitras.

Snowden sent an anonymous email to Glenn Greenwald saying, "I have sensitive documents that I would share with you."

Greenwald did not reply. So Snowden contacted Poitras.

In May, 2013, Snowden applied to Booz Allen for temporary leave so he could seek treatment for his epilepsy. Snowden flew from Hawaii to Hong Kong on May 2013, Within months, many newspaper carry news about the leaked documents. This sparked a huge public debate about the extent of government's spying.

The ongoing publications of leaked documents revealed that the US NSA was in close cooperation with the intelligence agencies of the UK, Australia, and Canada.. MSA was given a budget of $52 billion to buy data from private tech companies including Google and Yahoo.

Targets of information gathering included Brazil's oil giant Petrobas, UNICEF, Medicins du Monde, European Commissioner Joaquin Almunia, and the Israeli Prime Minister.

Snowden stayed in his room at Mira Hotel in Hong Kong and dare not venture out.. He engaged a Canadian human rights lawyer Robert Tibbo as his legal adviser. Snowden told the South China Morning Post that he would like to stay in Hong Kong for as long as he could if the government permit it. A Hong Kong rally occurred on June 15, 2013, giving Snowden its support.

Robert Tibbo arranged for Snowden to be housed in several locations to ensure his privacy and safety. On June 22, 2013, US officials revoked his US passport. Snowden flew out of Hong Kong the next day on Aeroflot SU213 to Moscow, accompanied by Sarah Harrison of Wikileaks.

The US government asked why the Hong Kong authorities did not detain Snowden. They replied that the papers were not cleared in time to stop Snowden from leaving Hong Kong.

In order to protect himself from being used by Russia, Snowden had no document on his person when he arrived in Moscow's Sheremetyevo Airport. The US authorities revoked his passport . So he was confined to the airport transit zone.

Sarah Harrison helped Snowden to seek asylum from 21 countries. Four countries offered Snowden permanent asylum: Ecuador, Nicaragua, Bolivia, and Venezuela. The US government told these four countries to hand over Snowden should he arrive at their country. Because of this, Snowden sought asylum from Russia.

The US government threatened the other countries that if they grant asylum to Snowden, the US government would not share intelligence with them. After 39 days confined to the airport transit zone, Russia granted asylum to Snowden. Wikileaks Assange told Snowden that he would be safest in Russia.

On June 14, 2013, US federal prosecutors filed a criminal complaint against Snowden, charging him with theft of government property and two counts of violating the Espionage Act of 1917 through unauthorized communication of national defense information and willful communication of classified information to an unauthorized person.

Each of the three charges carries a maximum possible prison term of ten years. The charge was initially secret. It was unsealed a week later.

Global reaction

Snowden is a 29-year-old American intelligence expert turned whistleblower. He copied and leaked highly classified information from the National Security Agency (NSA) in 2013.

Snowden was then working as a Central Intelligence Agency (CIA) employee and subcontractor based in Hawaii.

In 2013, Edward Snowden shocked the world when he revealed that the US government was secretly building a global mass surveillance system to collect every single phone call, text message, and email everywhere in the world.

Edward Snowden was involved in building this system, which was capable of prying into the private lives of every person on earth.

The data of our private lives were collected and stored on file, ready to be accessed by the US government not only now but potentially forever. Snowden felt that the US government had crossed the red line for him, and he decided to expose the truth at the risk of his liberty and even his life.

On June 8, 2013, Director of NSI James R Clapper denounced Snowden's disclosures of classified documents as reckless, doing huge, grave damage to the US intelligence capabilities.

Most of the initial reactions from members of Congress were negative. However, Gordon Humphrey, the conservative Republican senator for New Hampshire from 1979 - 1991, expressed his support for Snowden.

Humphrey contacted Snowden, saying that, provided he had not disclosed any document that would harm any intelligence agent, Snowden had done the right thing to expose what he regarded as massive violation of the United States Constitution.

Public opinion polls around the world are generally positive for Snowden as a courageous whistleblower.

For example, 50% of German polled considered Snowden a hero and 35% would hide him in their homes.

67% of Canadians polled considered Snowden a hero as did 60% of UK respondents.

There are more than ten memorable surveillance movies being made.

Eagle Eye is a movie about a super computer that thinks on its own. It aims to stage a coup to take over the government, using its control of traffic lights, machinery, banking system to direct activities.

Enemy of the State tels the story of Robert Dean, a Georgetown lawyer and family man who becomes the target of NSA harassment when a Congressman committed suicide. It is discovered that it is in fact a murder, and Dean is being set-up to take the blame. Dean finds an ally in security expert Edward Lyle to help him proves his innocence.

Another movie ***Minority Report*** tells the story of a future cop that works for the government's PreCrime Department. The department uses three psychic precogs that can predict who plans to commit murder, allowing John Aderton, the future cop to arrest the suspect before they kill. However, when Anderton himself is fingered as a suspect, he has to coax one of the precogs to help him unravel the problem.

China's surveillance system

Many countries are using AI technology as smart & safe city platforms. Some kind of surveillance system for building paper and digital profiles of individuals.

Companies supplying the most AI surveillance systems to other countries are Chinese companies such as Huawei, Hikvision, Dahua, and ZTE.

Companies from the US, France, Germany, Israel, and Japan are also supplying AI surveillance systems - IBM, Palantir and Cisco.

China has more CCTVs then the US and many other countries. China has a surveillance system. Its purpose, says the Chinese government, is to administer an electronic social credit system to guide people towards better behavior.

China's social credit system standardizes the assessment of citizens' and businesses' economic and social reputation or "social credit." It uses facial recognition and big data analysis technology. Paper records of individuals and households are also kept. This system is open to the public for searches.

Every citizen and every business is given 1,000 social credit points at the start.

Social credit points are deducted for such bad behavior as these:

Playing loud music
Eating in rapid transits
Jaywalking
Red light violations
No-show for hotel bookings
No-show for restaurant bookings
Unhygienic behavior
Using another person's transportation ID card.
Excessive online gambling

Children of untrustworthy people may be banned from attending private schools and even universities.

Social credit points will be earned by such good behavior as these:

Donating blood
Donating to charity
Volunteering for community services

People with high social credit ratings may receive rewards such as less waiting time at hospital and government agencies, discounts at hotels, and higher chance of getting job offers.

The National Development and Reform Commission of China reported in June 2019 that 26.82 million air tickets and 5.96 million high-speed rail tickets were denied to people blacklisted as untrustworthy.

4.37 million untrustworthy people have chosen to fulfill their duties required by law. It takes two to five years to be removed from the black list. This can be hastened when a person has done enough remedies.

Some personal details of blacklisted people may be made available online and also displayed in public places like movie theaters and buses.

Supporters of the social credit system claim that the system promote traditional values, regulate social behavior and thus improve the quality of life.

Critics of the social credit system claim that it has overstep the rights to privacy and reputation. Critics object to the government using it as a tool for comprehensive surveillance.

Cyber crime

Online fraud is now the most common crime in the world. You are ten times more likely to be a victim of an online fraud than a street robbery. You are vulnerable 24/7.

Your electronic equipment - mobile phone, computer, smart systems - can be both your friend and your foe. Your mobile phone can spy on you.

Cybercriminals - hackers and scammers - can rob you blind from the comfort of their air-conditioned homes.

Here are the security risks that you have to mitigate:

Unattended accounts, blogs, and websites - close them down

Human error - don't work online when you are tired; take a break

Third party apps - reduce the number of sources

Phishing attacks and scams - don't be impulsive; triple-confirm validity

Imposter accounts - again triple confirm validity

Malware attacks and hacks - create an online policy; install security technology

Unsecured mobile phone - lock your phone, report to police if lost or stolen

Here the 7 ways to protect yourself against cyber crime:

AVOID POPULAR SOCIAL MEDIA

Social media has made the world more connected. In most cases, that's a good thing. But there are hackers and scammers who can gain unauthorized access to your information and blackmail you.

Edward Snowden advises that if you care about your privacy and security, stay away from popular consumer Internet services such as Dropbox, Facebook, and Google.

Dropbox, Facebook and Google have improved their security. But that's not good enough. Encrypting while in transit is not secure enough. Data must be encrypted while still in your computer. That's why their competitors such as SpiderOak, RedPhone, and Silent Circle are more cyber-secure.

Crime-fighting agencies claim that encryption hurt the crime-fighting. Snowden dismisses such a claim saying that if they have sufficient grounds, they can get a warrant to gain access to the relevant data.

So the bottom line is to avoid Dropbox, Facebook, and Google. Choice their competitors such as SpiderOak, RedPhone, and Silent Circle.

PASSWORD

Your password must be unique. It must have at least 8 characters and symbols.

One way to help you remember your password is have a sentence, for example the title of a book:

When Corporations Rule The World

This will give you: WCRTW.

Then add a particular date of significance - for example - 1945 (end of World War II)

Then add a symbol, let's say @

So there you have it: WCRTW1945@

INSTALLING THE LATEST UPDATES

Don't procrastinate in installing updates as soon as it is available.

Updates of your operating system usually involve plugging any security risks.

BACKUP YOUR FILES

You need to regularly back up your file. Every operating system has its own back up facility. You can also download your important files into a device and keep it somewhere else.

If you don't back up your file, then you may lose your files forever, especially if there is a fire or cyber attack.

ONLINE POLICY

Organizations usually has a social media policy when they is using social media to do their marketing and public relations.

Usually, your public accountant has guidelines on creating a social media policy. All staff must be trained regularly on this policy. Access of social media must be limited to the most competent staff. A system of approval must be in place before a podcast is launched. Someone must be put in charge of the social media at all times. Regular audit must be made, maybe once a quarter. Install the latest cyber security technology.

It is a good idea for the most tech-savvy person to brief family and friends on the best practices as well.

SECURITY TECHNOLOGY

There is a cat and mouse game going on between data defenders and data thieves. So it is a great idea to keep abreast of the latest security technologies:

Hardware authentication. Username and password are not enough to stop malicious behavior. When one more element is added, the security is boosted - such as a one time password which will expire in two minutes.

User-behavior analytics. AI is able to detect malicious behavior and send an alert message to service provider who then contact the account user.

Data loss prevention. It is safest when data is encrypted while it is still in your computer.

Deep learning. Deep learning encompasses artificial intelligence and machine learning. Deep learning is able to observe what is normal behavior and what is suspicious behavior that is deviating from the norm.

The cloud. By transferring files to the cloud, the service provider can focus on boosting cyber security on a larger scale, pooling their resources.

Technological unemployment

Robots are changing our world. By year 2030, there will be 20 million robots in the world, 14 million of which will be in China.

Technological unemployment will be higher in low-skilled regions than in developed regions.

Automation and robots are saving businesses billions of dollars. However, millions of jobs will be lost to automation. New jobs will be created to supervise and maintain robots. This would require technical training. This in turn will affect education and unions as well.

The world will change in other areas as well. Prices of manufactured goods will be lower, savings can be translated into higher wages and better working conditions. And more tax revenue will be generated.

Construction projects can be completed in shorter time period. Here drones can take hundreds of aerial pictures to be fed into computers for analysis. 3-D animation will allow engineers to assess the work progress and spot any bottle necks and so forth.

This digital revolution has turbocharged globalization. Robots have taken over routine jobs. A 2018 Brookings Institution study that analyzed 28 industries in 18 OECD countries from 1970 to 2018 found that automation was responsible for holding down wages.

Although the Brookings study concluded that automation did not reduce the overall number of jobs available and even increased them, the study found that automation reduced the share of human labor in the value added to the work. Thus it had helped in wage growth.

In April 2018, Adair Turner, former Chairman of the Financial Services Authority and head of the Institute for New Economic Thinking, stated that it would already be possible to automate 50% of jobs with current technology, and that it will be possible to automate all jobs by 2060.

In 2017, South Korea became the most automated country on earth with one robot for every 19 employed humans. The government is considering changing the tax laws to provide disincentives to future automation increases.

Some form of universal basic income or a negative income tax may becoming increasingly essential and acceptable.

Funding such social programs may require a package of measures that will make holders of great wealth contribute more to society. This will mean addressing these devices of tax avoidance and evasion:

- Tax havens
- Bank secrecy
- Money laundering
- Regulatory arbitrage

Another issue that arises from technological unemployment is concerning the humanities. In the era of big data, the study of science, technology, engineering, and mathematics are pursued more vigorously than the humanities.

People are asking,

"Why should we still need to study the humanities in a STEM world?

Good question.

Humanities include subjects such as philosophy, language, literature, art, music, and religion.

Humans must control their destiny or robots will. Humanities will help us be more human, making human decisions. We must secure our cyber security or the robots will take over the world.

Can phones spy on you?

Whether Snowden is a hero or a traitor depends on whether what he reveals reflect the truth.

According to Edward Snowden, smartphones are an important way for government, tech companies, and bad actors to spy on you.

Because smartphones are everywhere, governments are focusing on smartphones to do bulk collection of data in their mass surveillance work. Whenever the phone is switched on, there's a digital record of your presence at that place.

As you go about your daily routine carrying your phone, you'll be using your phone to connect with the Internet and Wifi networks, using apps and so forth. You leave a digital trail which is recorded by the mass surveillance system. Such data is saved as valuable information which may become significant sometime in the future.

So long as the batteries are still in your phone, your phone may be accessed. So taking out your batteries for added security is a good idea. But some phones do not allow you to remove the batteries. Apple and iOS made it impossible to see what kind of network connections are constantly made on the device.

In 2014, academic Alexsandr Kogan and his company Global Science Research created an app called "thisisyourdigitallife." Users were paid to take a psychological test and the app collected the data. Participants were not aware of the consequences of their actions.

From the data collected from the participants, Kogan gained access to up to 50 million Facebook profiles. Kogan sold this bulk data to Cambridge Analytica. According to whistleblower Christopher Wylie, Cambridge Analytica used such data to develop psychographic profiles of people and deliver pro-Trump material to them online through social media to influence their votes.

Edward Snowden said that he would press the button that says "Do what I want but don't spy on me." But all the tech companies make sure such a button don't exist.

If tech companies and governments are sincere in ensuring the privacy of people, people must be given the option to disable any function that allow third parties to spy on them.

You have to make a decision.

Is the above explanation given by Edward Snowden valid?

If the above explanation is valid, then Edward Snowden is a HERO.

If the above explanation is invalid, then Edward Snowden is a TRAITOR.

Act now on your beliefs

Don't think that only authoritarian regimes spy on their citizens. Democratic governments also spy on their citizens. All governments need to know what's going on at ground level. We must ensure our own cyber security or robots will take over the world.

Can your mobile phone really spy on you, as explained by Edward Snowden?

If his explanation is valid, then he is a hero. If Edward Snowden is a hero in your eyes, then don't keep quiet. Speak up and support him as a brave whistleblower by whatever means at your disposal like social media, mainstream media, word of mouth and so forth.

Decisions have the power to steer and change your life forever. Therefore, nothing affects the quality of your life than your ability to make the right decisions. All that you have achieved or failed to achieved can be traced back to the decisions you've made - on issues concerning your vote, health, wealth, relationships, and life purpose.

Change your beliefs, and you will change your principles, values, virtues, habits, attitudes, social skills, ethics, behavior and so forth.

In life there are no mistakes, only lessons. The secret to resilience, happiness and a less stressful success is to avoid focusing on stagnant traits. Instead, focus on adopting an active, growth-oriented and problem-solving approach to life, and enjoying the journey together with your loved ones.

Here are the beliefs of greatness that will empower you to enjoy the journey with your loved ones:

- That which is hateful to you, do not do to your fellow human beings. Any interpretation of scriptures that bred hatred or disdain for others - whatever their beliefs - was illegitimate. (Hillel)
- True religion is protecting the powerless - orphans, widows, homeless, migrant workers, disabled, and injured soldiers re-

turning from an unnecessary war.

- Power without love is reckless and abusive. Love without power is sentimental and anemic. Power at its best is love implementing the demands of justice. Justice at its best is power correcting everything that stands against love. (Martin Luther King)

- That which matter most must never be at the mercy of things that matter least. (Goethe)

- Courage is not the absence of fear but rather the judgment that something is more important than fear. The brave may not live forever. But the cautious do not live at all. (Meg Cabot)

- So long as you open your heart to beauty, hope, cheer, courage and power, so long are you young. (Samuel Ulman). I know of no more encouraging fact than the unquestionable ability of man to elevate his life by conscious endeavor (Henry David Thoreau).

- We should encourage each other to follow the rules of considerate conduct such as think before we act, listen more, argue less, seek first to understand, think twice before asking favors, avoid shifting responsibility and blame, avoid jumping to conclusions, respect other's opinion, and enjoying the journey with your loved ones.

- If you want to achieve what you've never achieved before, you have to grow to become what you've never become before. (Brian Tracy). Insanity is doing the same over and over again and expecting different results. No problem can be solved at the same level of consciousness that created it. (Albert Einstein)

- Success and cheerfulness in life are not the result of what we have but rather how we live. What we do with the things we already have now makes the biggest difference in the quality of our life. (Tony Robbins)

- Studies have shown that companies hire for attitude and train for skills. (Singapore Airlines).
- Humility is the beginning of wisdom. (Zen habits)
- A foolish definition of success is the attainment of a certain amount of money, power, and privilege. A wise definition of success is enjoying the journey of lifelong learning with your loved ones.
- All men are created equal, endowed with the unalienable rights to life, liberty and the pursuit of happiness. (US Declaration of Independence)
- The world will be safer and prosperous when all nations adhere to the principles of peaceful coexistence where there is mutual respect for each other's territorial sovereignty and the right to self-determination and non-interference. (China-India)
- Whether a cat is black or white makes no difference. A cat that catches mice is a good cat. Whether we label an ideology socialism, capitalism, communism, or authoritarianism makes no difference. A government that can provide affordable subsidized public housing, meaningful jobs, efficient transport system, clean environment, fantastic schools, universal health care, recreation centers, and national security is a good government and should be given a strong mandate to govern. (Deng Xiaoping)
- Every nation must strive to avoid contracting the national disease of schizophrenia where there are two equally dominant sectarian political parties, bickering with each other like two juveniles. It is best if there is a political party that promote universal values that protect the rights of minorities so as to gain at least 70% of popular vote thus attaining a strong mandate to govern.

- Workers must enjoy democracy at the workplace where they have a say in the management of the company and reserve the right to buy the company if the owners decide to sell.
- All citizens must have a fair share in the prosperity of the nation. This can be achieved by practicing universal basic income (UBI) calculated as a small percentage of the living wage. UBI is able to soften the ills of neoliberalism by reducing the pain and frustration of the underprivileged who are the victims of the wealth gap between the rich and the poor. UBI is able to reduce the risk of violent civil unrest.
- Every citizen must be given universal healthcare.
- Every person has the right to demand privacy, especially when he or she has not committed any crime. (Edward Snowden)
- Every person has the right to choose his own way of life without being judged or criticized so long as he or she respects the rule of law. He can choose voluntary simplicity, country living, living off the grid, any profession, urban competition, climbing the corporate ladder, activism, the military, or politics.
- Whistleblowers should be protected by law when they expose the wrongdoings within the company or government.

You'll never walk alone

As we said in the beginning, we'll say it at the end. We are inspired to take action by the same emotions because we are fellow human beings.

Even though we are enjoying the journey, in an odyssey of lifelong learning from our mistakes, be prepared for a long bumpy ride. Therefore, be prepared to tough it out to the very end through thick and thin, through wind and rain.

Never ever give up part way. If you are already halfway there, don't ever turn around and go back. Press on with hope in your heart and you'll never walk alone, for we are with you all the way:

Former president Calvin Coolidge says it best:

Nothing can take the place of ***PERSISTENCE.***
Talent will not.
Nothing is as common as unsuccessful people with talent.
Genius will not.
Unrewarded genius is almost a proverb.
Education will not.
The world is full of educated derelicts.
*The slogan "****PRESS ON!****" has solved and always will solve*
The problems of the human race.

To help you keep going when the going gets tough, always remember that ***you'll never walk alone***. Hum this song, and soon others who are sharing the same pain and struggles of life as you, will join you in spirit, in song, and in taking action to pursue the same VISION OF A BETTER WORLD!

You'll Never Walk Alone is a show tune from the 1945 Rodgers

& Hammerstein musical ***Carousel***. In the second act of the musical, Nettie Fowler, the cousin of the protagonist Julie Jordan, sings ***"You'll Never Walk alone"*** to comfort and encourage Julie when her husband, Billy Bigelow, the male lead, falls on his knife and dies after a failed robbery attempt.

In the final scene of ***Carousel***, in the commencement ceremony, Louise (Billy and Julie's daughter) remain quiet and sad even when the audience was singing the song. The now invisible Billy was granted a chance to return to earth for this one special day to redeem himself and silently motivate his daughter, the unhappy Louise, to join in the song. Sudden she felt that rush of courage and she join in to sing ***You'll Never Walk Alone.***

This song, ***You'll Never Walk Alone,*** inspire so much emotions that it is sung almost everywhere - in concerts, Emmy Awards nights, anniversaries and of course in association football clubs like Liverpool, Dortmund, Celtics, FC Twente, Feyenoord, SC Canbuur, Club Brugge and so forth.

*Here's the lyrics of **You'll Never Walk Alone:***

When you walk through a storm
Hold your head up high
And don't be afraid of the dark.
At the end of a storm
There's a golden sky
And the sweet silver song of a lark.
Walk on through the wind
Walk on through the rain
Though your dreams be tossed and blown.
Walk on, walk on
With hope in your heart
And you'll never walk alone.

You'll never walk alone.
Walk on, walk on
With hope in your heart
And you'll never walk alone
You'll never walk alone.

Your loved ones who have gone to heaven are whispering in your heart, encouraging you to PRESS ON to fight until the war is won.

The best rendition, in my view, is by Gerry and the Pacemakers YouTube video:

Gerry & the Pacemaker - You'll Never Walk Alone (Official video)

The race set before us

Jesus of Nazareth was a first century Jewish preacher and religious leader during the reign of Augustus Caesar of the Roman empire.

Jesus is the central figure of Christianity and Islam. Jesus debated with fellow Jews on how best to follow God. He was the wisest and the kindest of men. He was kind to the poor but fierce with those who make money out of religion.

Jesus had a tremendous following. Both Roman and Jewish leaders felt threatened by his popularity. To get rid of Jesus, the Jewish leaders accused Jesus of blasphemy and rebellion against Rome. The plotters agitated the crowd to call for his arrest and execution. Pontius Pilate washed his hands, claiming that it was the Jews who wanted him dead. He was crucified on a wooden cross at Golgotha.

Years later, his disciples and followers spread his religion. Apostle Paul made it into an organized religion. It grew to become a political force in Europe. The Catholic Church has 1.7 billion baptized members.

At the time of Martin Luther (1483 - 1546), a Roman Catholic priest in Germany, many believers were already disillusioned by abuses and malpractices of the church. On October 31, 1517, Luther rose to the front of the Reformation when he posted his "Ninety-Five Theses" on the main door of the castle church in Wittenberg.

Charles V, Emperor of the Roman empire, ordered Luther to retract his theology before a council of princes, nobles, and clergymen in Worms, Germany. Before them, Luther refused, saying:

Unless I am convinced by the testimony of the Scriptures or by clear reason (for I do not trust either in the pope or in the councils alone, since it is known that they have often erred and contradicted themselves), I am bound by the Scriptures I have quoted and my conscience is captive to the Word of God. I cannot and I will not retract anything, since it is neither safe nor right to go against conscience. I cannot do otherwise.

Here are the names of those brave souls who stood up for what is right and proper down the ages:

Martin Luther (against religious abuse of power)
Alexander Hamilton (fought against slavery)
Martin Luther King (rights of blacks)
Deng Xiaoping (reformation of communism)
Lee Kuan Yew (gold standard of governance)

Claus von Stuufenberg (plot to assassinate Hitler)
Jack Abramoff (exposed fraudulent lobbying)
Daniel Ellsberg (exposed illegal activities of warmongers)
Julian Assange (advocated transparency)
Edward Snowden (fought for privacy against surveillance)
Christopher Wylie (exposed wrongdoing of Cambridge Analytica)

Zhu Ruifeng (exposed wrongdoing of Chinese officials)
Sandra Martinez Cam (exposed wrongdoing of Philippines officials)
Anat Kamm (exposed wrongdoing of Israeli Defense Force)
Xavier Justo (exposed corruption in 1MDB scandal in Malaysia)

Eliot Ness (brought Al Capone to justice)
Frank Serpico (clean cop who survived assassination attempt)
Michael Franzese (NY mafia capo turned good guy)
Katharine Gun (exposed US/UK lies about Iraq)
Mark Felt (exposed FBI wrongdoing)
Thomas Drake (exposed NSA wrongdoing)
James Paris (exposed CIA wrongdoing)

John Doe (exposed off-shore accounts at Mossack Fonseca)
Matthew Lee (exposed accounting fraud at Lehman Brothers)
Eileen Foster (exposed mortgage fraud at Countrywide)
Edward O'Donnel (exposed fraud at Bank of America))
Sherron Watkins (exposed accounting fraud at Enron)
Carmen Segarra (exposed noncompliance by Goldman Sachs)
Alyne Fleischman (exposed white collar fraud at JP Morgan)
Andrew Macguire (exposed gold price manipulation at JP Morgan)
Richard Bowell III (exposed fraud at Citigroup)
Tyler Schultz (exposed fraud at Theranos)
David Korten (exposed human tragedy from globalization)
Carson Block (market short on fraudulent companies)
Sheelah Kolhatkar (exposed Wall Street cheats)
Cynthia Cooper (exposed fraud at World.com)
Harry Markopolos (exposed Madoff's Ponzi scheme)
Wendell Pottner (exposed fraud by insurer CIGNA)

David Rosenhan (exposed psychiatry as a fake science)
Jeffrey Wigand (exposed fraud at tobacco company)
Jim Wetta (exposed fraud at AstraZeneca)
Cheryl Eckhardt (exposed fraud at GlaxoSmithKline)
John Kochinski (exposed fraud at Pfizer marketing Bextra)

Peter Frost (exposed wrongdoing at Pfizer)

Anita Roddick (protecting small producers)
Muhammad Yunus (affirmed creditworthiness of the poor)
Richard Wolff (installing democracy at work)
Chris Hedges (anti-war anti-oligarch activist)
Martin Jaques (exposed American myopia)
Chelsea Handler (protecting the common man)
Malala Yousafzai (educating girls in Pakistan)
Mina Mangai (advocating woman rights in Afghanistan)
Linda Masarira (advocating woman rights in Zimbabwe)
Greta Thunberg (Save the earth, from Sweden)

Whistleblowers (exposing fraud)
NGOs (promoting social responsibility)
Advocates for natural cures (fighting against drug pushers)
Investigative reporters (seeking truth from facts)
Defense lawyers (protecting whistleblowers)
And all other activists around the world who strive for a world without corruption.

Therefore, since we are surrounded by such a great cloud of witnesses, let us brush aside all the trivial things that distract us. Let us run without waver, the race that is set before us, to fight for justice and equality. Be the change you want to see in the world!

In life, there are NO MISTAKES, ONLY LESSONS!

Enjoy the journey with your loved ones!

This is true success!

About the author

Pendragon Tim Chng is a leading contributor to QUORA, a question and answer forum in the Internet. He has authored eight other books through Amazon Kindle Create. He holds a B.Sc. (Hons) from the University of Manitoba, Canada and M.Sc. (Science education) from the University of Wisconsin, USA. He lives in Singapore with his beloved wife ***Mui Ann*** and four wonderful children, ***Christopher, Jonathan, Veronica***, and ***Yvonne***.

Pendragon Tim Chng takes this opportunity to thank ***Lok Vi Meng, Senior Counsel and Partner at Rodyk & Davidson, Singapore***. Vi Meng had given moral support to PTC when he needed it most.

www.ingramcontent.com/pod-product-compliance
Lightning Source LLC
Chambersburg PA
CBHW030610220526
45463CB00004B/1245

* 9 7 8 1 6 7 0 5 3 0 2 3 3 *